Rigor for Students with Special Needs

Barbara R. Blackburn and Bradley S. Witzel

Routledge
Taylor & Francis Group

LONDON AND NEW YORK

First published 2014 by Eye on Education

Published 2014 by Routledge
2 Park Square, Milton Park, Abingdon, Oxon OX14 4RN
711 Third Avenue, New York, NY, 10017, USA

Routledge is an imprint of the Taylor & Francis Group, an informa business

Library of Congress Cataloging-in-Publication Data

Blackburn, Barbara R., 1961–
Rigor for students with special needs / Barbara R. Blackburn and Bradley S.
Witzel.
     pages   cm
Includes bibliographical references.
ISBN 978-1-59667-248-2
1. Children with disabilities—Education—United States.
2. Youth with disabilities—Education—United States.
3. Motivation in education—United States.
4. Classroom environment—United States.
5. Academic achievement—United States.
I. Title.
LC4031.B488 2013
371.910430973—dc23   2013007231

ISBN 13: 978-1-59667-248-2 (pbk)

Copyeditor: Sarah Chassé
Designer and Compositor: Matthew Williams, click! Publishing Services
Cover Designer: Dave Strauss, 3FoldDesign

Also Available from Eye On Education

Rigor Is Not a Four-Letter Word, Second Edition
Barbara R. Blackburn

Rigor Made Easy: Getting Started
Barbara R. Blackburn

Rigor in Your School: A Toolkit for Leaders
Ronald Williamson and Barbara R. Blackburn

Rigorous Schools and Classrooms: Leading the Way
Ronald Williamson and Barbara R. Blackburn

Classroom Motivation from A to Z:
How to Engage Your Students in Learning
Barbara R. Blackburn

Classroom Instruction from A to Z: How to Promote Student Learning
Barbara R. Blackburn

Differentiation Is an Expectation:
A School Leader's Guide to Building a Culture of Differentiation
Kimberly K. Hewitt and Daniel K. Weckstein

How the Best Teachers Differentiate Instruction
Elizabeth Breaux and Monique Boutte Magee

Differentiating by Student Interest: Strategies and Lesson Plans
Joni Turville

Differentiating by Student Learning Preferences:
Strategies and Lesson Plans
Joni Turville

RTI Strategies that Work in the K–2 Classroom
RTI Strategies that Work in the 3–6 Classroom
Eli Johnson and Michelle Karns

Improving Adolescent Literacy: An RTI Implementation Guide
Pamela S. Craig and Rebecca K. Sarlo

Teach Me, I Dare You
Judith Allen Brough, Sherrel Bergmann, and Larry C. Holt

The Principal as Student Advocate:
A Guide for Doing What's Best for All Students
M. Scott Norton, Larry K. Kelly, and Anna R. Battle

Meet the Authors

Dr. Barbara Blackburn has dedicated her life to raising the level of rigor and motivation for professional educators and students alike. What differentiates Barbara's books are her easily executable concrete examples based on decades of experience as a teacher, professor, and consultant. Barbara's dedication to education was inspired in her early years by her parents. Her father's doctorate and lifetime career as a professor taught her the importance of professional training. Her mother's career as school secretary shaped Barbara's appreciation of the effort all staff play in the education of every child.

Barbara has taught early childhood, elementary, middle, and high school students and has served as an educational consultant for three publishing companies. She holds a master's degree in school administration and is certified as a teacher and school principal in North Carolina. She received her Ph.D. in Curriculum and Teaching from the University of North Carolina at Greensboro. In 2006, she received the award for Outstanding Junior Professor at Winthrop University. She recently left her position at the University of North Carolina at Charlotte to write and speak full time.

In addition to speaking at state and national conferences, she also regularly presents workshops for teachers and administrators in elementary, middle, and high schools. Her workshops are lively and engaging and filled with practical information. Her most popular topics include:

♦ Rigor Is NOT a Four-Letter Word

♦ Rigorous Schools and Classrooms: Leading the Way

♦ Motivation + Engagement + Rigor = Student Success

♦ Instructional Strategies that Motivate Students

♦ Content Literacy Strategies for the Young and the Restless

♦ Motivating Yourself and Others

♦ Engaging Instruction Leads to Higher Achievement

♦ High Expectations and Increased Support Lead to Success

Bradley Witzel, Ph.D., started his career as a paraeducator assisting in classrooms with students with severe disabilities. As an experienced classroom teacher, he mainly taught high achieving students with disabilities and at-risk concerns. He currently serves as an associate professor and program coordinator at Winthrop University, the flagship education college for the state of South Carolina.

Brad has written several books, including *Solving Equations, Building Number Sense through the Common Core*, and the bestseller *RTI in Math*. In addition, he has written several dozen research and practitioner articles, book chapters, and numerous training manuals. He has delivered several hundred workshops and conference presentations and currently works with school districts to improve student performance scores. He is an elected member of the Smarter Balanced Assessment Consortium (SBAC) Accessibility and Accommodations work group and of the Governing Board of the Southeast Regional Educational Laboratory (REL), funded by the Institute of Education Sciences (IES).

Brad currently serves as the editor of *Focus on Inclusive Education* through the Association of Childhood Education International (ACEI) and recently served as a panelist on the IES practice guide *Assisting Students Struggling with Mathematics* and as an invited reviewer of the final report from the National Mathematics Advisory Panel. Most importantly, he is a father of two, husband of an educator, and son of two educators.

To my sister, Becky, who loves children and
dedicates her life to Matthew and Jenna.
—Barbara

To my wife, Isabelle, and daughters Laura and Caroline,
thank you for your support of my many projects. I love you.
—Brad

Acknowledgments

From Barbara and Brad:
Thank you to

- ♦ Lauren Davis and the Eye On Education staff for their help;
- ♦ Dave Strauss for his great cover design;
- ♦ Matthew Williams for designing the text;
- ♦ Jennifer L. Jones, Ann Linson, Amber Tos, and Rebecca Yellets for reviewing the book and helping us make it even better;
- ♦ Melissa Miles for her editing support; and
- ♦ Kendra Alston for her help with the Book Club and Study Group Guide.

From Barbara:
Thank you to my family and friends for their continuing support.

From Brad:
To all of my students, you have taught me far more than I ever taught you.

Supplemental Downloads

Many of the tools discussed and displayed in this book are also available on the Routledge website as Adobe Acrobat files. Permission has been granted to purchasers of this book to download these tools and print them.

You can access these downloads by visiting www.routledge.com/9781596672482 and clicking on the Free Downloads tab.

Table of Contents

Introduction

This book, *Rigor for Students with Special Needs,* is a work that is five years in the making. Barbara began writing about rigor in the classroom in 2008, and one of the most often asked questions has been, "But how does that apply to students with special needs?" She also heard from some teachers that their mainstreamed students simply "couldn't handle the current work, much less additional rigor."

We (Barbara and Brad) were colleagues at Winthrop University at the time and often had discussions on this very topic. Ultimately, we decided to write a book that addressed this question, especially for teachers who are trying to balance the varying needs of students in their classrooms.

As you read through the chapters, you'll find information about what rigor is and isn't. Then we'll turn our attention to issues around student motivation. Next, you'll read about student expectations, supporting students' needs, and assessing learning. Finally, we'll address working with parents and Individualized Education Programs (IEPs). (Note: We use the term Individualized Education Programs as it is termed in the federal register. However, IEPs are also commonly referred to as Individualized Education Plans, because, as plans, they should be reviewed regularly to determine success or needed adjustments.) Throughout, you'll find practical applications, stories from our experiences, and the voices of teachers and students.

We hope you will view reading the book as a journey that will help you and your students rise to new levels of rigor. Please contact us with your stories and experiences; we are always interested in hearing from teachers and students. We both regularly work with schools and districts on issues related to rigor and students with special needs. Brad specializes in math; Barbara, in literacy. Barbara can be reached at bcgroup@gmail.com or through her website at www.barbarablackburnonline.com. Brad may be reached at witzelb@winthrop.edu or through his website at coe.winthrop.edu/witzelb.

1

The What and Why of Rigor

This book is designed to help teachers meet the needs of students with high-incidence disabilities (e.g., learning disabilities, emotional disabilities, etc.) who are included in general-education classrooms. The number-one question we are asked during our work with teachers is, "Can instruction and learning be rigorous for students with special needs too?" The answer is a resounding yes.

1. Students with High-Incidence Disabilities
2. Why Does Rigor Matter?
3. Myths About Rigor
4. Defining Rigor

Students with High-Incidence Disabilities

Approximately 3 percent to 6 percent of all school-age children and adolescents are believed to have developmental reading disabilities. In fact, almost 50 percent of children receiving special education have learning disabilities. Because of this, there is a broad base of research and strategies we can use to help students learn at higher levels.

United States numbers according to the National Center for Education Statistics (2010)

Percent with disabilities	13.1	Total number of students with disabilities	6,481,000
Percent with learning disabilities	4.9	Total number of students with learning disabilities	2,431,000
Percent with emotional disabilities	0.9	Total number of students with emotional disabilities	463,000
Percent with intellectual disabilities	0.8	Total number of students with intellectual disabilities	407,000

Today, many students struggle to acquire literacy and mathematics skills in our current standards-based approach. Concern about this issue has given rise to educational models such as Response to Intervention (RtI), which includes multiple layers of instructional and curricular approaches to help meet the needs of students, labeled or not, throughout each school.

Key Statistics

The overall dropout rate for students without disabilities is approximately 11% (U.S. Department of Education, 2001).
"Students with emotional/behavioral disorders have a dropout rate between 50% and 59% while between 32% and 36% of students with learning disabilities drop out of school" (Kemp, 2006, 236).
Over 80% of those in jail dropped out of high school (Office of Juvenile Justice and Delinquency Prevention, 1995).
"More than 60% of prison inmates have learning disabilities" (Pitt, 2003).

While these statistics seem frightening, they are a reminder that we need to work hard and smart early in children's lives and sustain our efforts to make a long-term effect. Additionally, a critical fact remains: just because a student is labeled learning disabled or at risk, it does not mean he or she is incapable of learning. Students with learning disabilities have average to above-average intelligence. Therefore, ensuring their success in school is a matter of finding the appropriate teaching strategies and motivation tools, all of which we can control as teachers.

 A Reflective Moment

Which of your students have learning disabilities? Do you agree that since students with learning disabilities have average to above-average intelligence, their lack of success is not due to inability?

_____

_____

Why Does Rigor Matter?

Rigor is creating an environment in which each student is expected to learn at high levels, each student is supported so he or she can learn at high levels, and each student demonstrates learning at high levels. (Blackburn, 2008)

Many teachers say they care about rigor because they are told they have to. When asked why we care about rigor, our response is simple. There are a variety of reasons, such as the clear research base that shows students need more rigor, the new Common Core State Standards (CCSS) and updated state standards that require more rigor, and, most convincing, the number of students who graduate from high school ill-prepared for college or the workforce. Ultimately, rigor is about helping students learn at higher levels, and that's why we became teachers.

Barbara was reminded of this a few years ago when she was in a school and met a student named Gabrielle. Barbara's favorite question to ask students is, "If you were in charge of the school, what would you change?" Gabrielle's answer was insightful. She said, "For people who don't understand as much . . . [they should] be in higher-level classes to understand more [because] if they already don't know much, you don't want to teach them to not know much over and over." Now, you might laugh at her comment, but it is very true. Many students aren't really progressing; they are learning variations of the same things, or they are not learning at all. This is especially true for students with special needs included in a general-education classroom.

 **A Reflective Moment**

Why does rigor matter to you?

_____

_____

Myths About Rigor

Before we look at what rigor is, let's take a moment to look at the myths that distract from true rigor.

Five Myths About Rigor
1. Lots of homework is a sign of rigor.
2. Rigor means doing more.
3. Rigor is not for everyone.
4. Providing support means lessening rigor.
5. Resources equal rigor.

Myth #1: Lots of Homework Is a Sign of Rigor

For many people, the best indicator of rigor is the amount of homework required of students. Some teachers pride themselves on the amount of homework they assign, and there are parents who judge teachers by homework quantity.

Realistically, all homework is not equally useful. Some of it is just busywork, assigned by teachers because principals or parents expect it. One study (Wasserstein, 1995) found that students described busywork as unimportant and, therefore, not satisfying. Contrary to what many adults believe, students viewed hard work as important, and they enjoyed the challenge and sense of pride that went with accomplishing a task that was hard.

Homework, if timed incorrectly, can do worse than bore; it could lead to incorrect understanding. This is not an indictment of homework but rather of how it is often used. Homework should be considered independent practice. Assigning homework before students understand a concept or procedure will result in students giving up on the assignment, seeking help from others who may or may not understand what to do, or even guessing as to how to complete the work. Thus, students must understand what, why, and how before homework is assigned. Homework should consist of items and questions that students have sufficient background to complete accurately and with meaning.

Amount and type of work should both be considered before homework is assigned. For some students, doing a high quantity of homework leads to burnout. When that occurs, students are less likely to complete homework and may be discouraged about any learning activity. More work often means doing more low-level activities, frequently repetitions of things already learned. Such narrow and rigid approaches to learning do not define a rigorous classroom. Students learn in many different ways. Just as instruction must vary to meet the individual needs of students, so must homework. Rigorous and challenging learning experiences will vary with the student. Their designs will vary, as will their duration. Ultimately, it is the quality of the assignment that makes a difference in terms of rigor.

Myth #2: Rigor Means Doing More

Many parents and educators believe that a rigorous classroom is characterized by requiring students to do more than they currently do, and that rigor is defined by the content of a lesson, the number of problems assigned, the amount of reading, or the number of requirements.

True rigor is expecting every student to learn and perform at high levels, even higher than they are currently achieving. This requires instruction that allows students to delve deeply into their learning, to engage in critical-thinking and problem-solving activities, to be curious and imaginative, and to demonstrate agility and adaptability (Wagner, 1999). Simply put, more is not necessarily better, especially when more includes only repetitive low level tasks that are not designed to build mastery. This belief is not counter to practice, which is an incredibly valuable step in the learning process. Rather, providing redundant tasks not intended to improve learning or help students retain information is simply asking them to complete work that fills a time gap, not a learning gap.

Myth #3: Rigor Is Not for Everyone

Some teachers think the only way to assure success for everyone is to lower standards and lessen rigor. This may mask a hidden belief that some students can't really learn at high levels. You may have heard of the Pygmalion effect: students live up to or down to our expectations of them.

We were recently working with a school that had one solution for increasing rigor—putting all students in advanced classes. That may be an option, but we're not convinced there is only one way to increase rigor for all students. First, although the intention is excellent, not all students are ready for an advanced class without extra support. Second, that choice sends the message that the only teachers capable of rigorous instruction are those who teach advanced students. We know from our own experience as teachers of students who perform far below their grade level that any teacher can be rigorous, and any student can reach higher levels with the right support. In fact, that is the exact purpose of this book—to show you how to provide rigorous instruction within your classroom to those students with special needs.

Myth #4: Providing Support Means Lessening Rigor

In the United States, we believe in rugged individualism. We are to pull ourselves up by our bootstraps and do things on our own. Working in teams or accepting help is often seen as a sign of weakness. However, supporting students so they can learn at high levels is central to the definition of rigor. As teachers design lessons that move students toward more challenging work, they must provide scaffolding to support them as they learn.

Ron Williamson, coauthor of books on leadership and rigor, asked teachers and parents about their experience with rigor. Both groups repeatedly told stories of how successful they were on rigorous tasks when they felt a high level of support—a safety net. Often, people described tasks at which they were initially not successful. Only after additional time or effort did they experience success. In fact, many people said they would not have been successful without strong support.

The same is true for students. They are motivated to do well when they value what they are doing, and when they believe that they have a chance of success. The most successful classrooms and schools are those that build a culture of success, celebrate success, and create a success mentality.

Myth #5: Resources Equal Rigor

Another common refrain is: "If we bought this program or textbook or technology, then we would be rigorous." We've worked for and with multiple publishing companies, and we have learned a critical lesson: it's never the resources; it's always how you use them. Mediocre materials in the hands of a great teacher are effective. Excellent material used by a poor teacher provides minimal results. And excellent materials with an excellent teacher can work wonders.

The right resources can certainly help increase the rigor in your classroom. Resources reviewed by What Works Clearinghouse as well as those of independent research groups, such as Mathematica Policy Research, the Center on Instruction, and the National Science Foundation often reveal strengths and weaknesses of different strategies that inform educators what and how to help students. However, raising the level of rigor for your students is not entirely dependent on the resources you have.

A Reflective Moment

Which myth resonates with you? Why?

_____

_____

Defining Rigor

Barbara's definition of rigor has a sharp focus on instruction. In her book *Rigor Is Not a Four-Letter Word*, she defines rigor as creating an environment in which

- each student is expected to learn at high levels
- each student is supported so he or she can learn at high levels
- each student demonstrates learning at high levels

Notice we are looking at the environment you create. The trifold approach to rigor is not limited to the curriculum students are expected to learn. It is more than a specific lesson or instructional strategy. It is deeper than what a student says or does in response to a lesson. True rigor is the result of weaving together all elements of schooling to raise students to higher levels of learning. Let's take a deeper look at the three aspects of the definition.

Expecting Students to Learn at High Levels

The first component of rigor is creating an environment in which each student is expected to learn at high levels. Having high expectations starts with the recognition that every student possesses the potential to succeed at his or her individual level.

Almost every teacher or leader we talk with says, "We have high expectations for our students." Sometimes that is evidenced by the behaviors in the school; other times, however, faculty actions don't match the words. There are concrete ways to implement and assess rigor in classrooms.

As you design lessons that incorporate more rigorous opportunities for learning, you will want to consider the questions that are embedded in the instruction. High-level questioning is an integral part of a rigorous classroom. Look for open-ended questions, ones that are at the higher levels of Bloom's Taxonomy (analysis, synthesis). You'll find more on questioning in Chapter Three.

A Reflective Moment

Take thirty minutes to monitor your questions. How many of your questions are at high levels? How many require one-word answers?

_____

_____

It is also important to pay attention to how you respond to student questions. When we visit schools, it is not uncommon to see teachers who ask high-level questions. But for whatever reason, we then see some of the same teachers accept low-level responses from students. In rigorous classrooms, teachers push students to respond at high levels. They ask extending questions. Extending questions are questions that encourage students to explain their reasoning and think through ideas. When a student does not know the immediate answer but has sufficient background information to provide a response to a question, the teacher continues to probe and guide the student's thinking rather than moving on to the next student. Insist on thinking and problem solving.

 Avoid the Roadblock!

Addressing poor academic performance may be uncomfortable for students who are accustomed to being ignored in class. Students who are used to failing may give up on learning in school. Instead, they find other less productive things to do with their time. Lack of knowledge is acceptable, but lack of effort is not. Encourage participation and academic engagement during class activities. Consistent encouragement and exchanges can change a class culture and help build students' self-esteem.

Supporting Students to Learn at High Levels

High expectations are important, but the most rigorous schools assure that each student is supported so he or she can learn at high levels, which is the second part of the definition. It is essential that teachers design lessons that move students to more challenging work while simultaneously providing ongoing scaffolding to support students' learning as they move to those higher levels.

Providing additional scaffolding throughout lessons is one of the most important ways to support your students, whether diagnosed with learning disabilities or not. Often, students with disabilities have the ability or knowledge to accomplish a task but are overwhelmed at the complexity of it, therefore getting lost in the process. This can occur in a variety of ways, but it requires that teachers ask themselves during every step of their lessons, "What extra support might my students need?" In Chapter Four, we'll explore this in more detail.

Examples of Scaffolding Strategies

- asking guiding questions
- chunking information
- highlighting or color coding steps in a project
- writing standards as questions for students to answer
- using visuals and graphic organizers, such as a math graphic organizer for word problems, maps to accompany history lessons, or color-coded paragraphs to help students make meaning of texts

---

Ensuring Students Demonstrate Learning at High Levels

The third component of a rigorous classroom is providing each student with opportunities to demonstrate learning at high levels. A teacher recently said to us, "If we provide more challenging lessons that include extra support, then learning will happen." What we've learned is that if we want students to show us they understand what they learned at a high level, we need to provide opportunities for students to demonstrate they have truly mastered that learning. In order for students to demonstrate their learning, they must first be engaged in academic tasks.

Student engagement is a critical aspect of rigor. In too many classrooms, most of the instruction consists of teacher-centered, large-group instruction, perhaps in an interactive lecture or discussion format. The general practice during these lessons is for the teacher to ask a question and then call on a student to respond. While this provides an opportunity for one student to demonstrate understanding, the remaining students don't do so. Students with special needs are particularly likely to not respond.

A better option would be for the teacher to allow all students to pair-share, respond with thumbs-up or thumbs-down, write their answers on small whiteboards and share their answers, or use handheld computers that tally the responses. (See the table that follows.) Such activities hold each student accountable for demonstrating his or her understanding. We'll explore this concept further in Chapter Five: Demonstration of Student Learning (Assessment).

A Reflective Moment

How engaged are your students?

_____

_____

Indicators of Student Engagement Level

Low Engagement	*High Engagement*
◆ Few students respond. ◆ Two or three students discuss content with teacher. ◆ Students are asked if they understand, and they answer with a simple yes or no, with no probing.	◆ All students respond. ◆ All students discuss content in small groups. ◆ All students write responses in journals or on exit slips.

 Avoid the Roadblock!

We understand that you face a variety of challenges, including pressure from standardized testing, parents, accountability, and teacher evaluations tied to test scores. It is important to realize that using the strategies we are recommending help you and your students make progress toward higher grades, which is a concern for parents, as well as scoring at a more advanced level on state tests. You will find that progress is slow but steady when you focus on best instructional practices.

If creating a more rigorous classroom seems a bit overwhelming, remember that it is a journey, one that continues as you and your students learn and grow and change. Please remember that there is no magic formula for increasing rigor. It's a process of continually adjusting your expectations, instruction, and assessments to ensure that each of your students learns at higher and higher levels.

We know you will be successful in your journey to enhance the level of rigor your students with special needs experience. The fact that you are reading this book means you continue to learn, and that is at the heart of rigor. Expect the best, but accept that no one is perfect. In the end, you will have made a difference to students.

Summary

♦ Students with learning disabilities struggle to acquire literacy and mathematics skills in our current standards-based approach.

♦ A rigorous environment and curriculum challenge all students to reach their full potential.

♦ Rigor does not mean extra work, additional resources, or more practice with the same skill. Rather, it involves high teacher expectations, scaffolding, and varied opportunities to demonstrate understanding.

2

Motivating Students

Students' lack of motivation is one of the key roadblocks to helping learning-disabled students succeed in a rigorous environment. While improved and informed instruction provides new opportunities for students to succeed, all too often students do not accept these opportunities, especially those with learning disabilities. Hampered by feelings of frustration and failure, a student may feel helpless to turn around his or her academic performance.

1. Connecting Intrinsic and Extrinsic Motivation
2. Motivating through Extrinsic Means
3. Motivating through Intrinsic Means
4. Looking Beneath the Surface

When a student has experienced frustration and failure for a long time, the student may prematurely conclude what he or she can and cannot do. Some students turn their efforts to unproductive social and academic behaviors instead of continuing to strive for success. In such situations, educators must employ motivation principles to enable students to make better choices.

Motivation can be extrinsic or intrinsic. Intrinsic motivation takes place when a person feels internally satisfied during or after a behavior (Sprick, Garrison, & Howard, 1998). If intrinsically motivated, a student will repeat a task regardless of external stimuli supporting or reprimanding his or her behavior. Intrinsic motivation is rare, since there are many competing stimuli surrounding a behavior. The competing stimuli are extrinsic. Extrinsic motivation takes place when someone engages in a certain behavior to reach satisfying consequences outside of the person during and/or after the behavior.

Take for example two Special Olympics volunteers. Volunteer 1 repeatedly offers to help regardless of how she is treated while helping. The motivation for her is intrinsic to her desire to help. Volunteer 2, however, repeatedly offers to help because of the appreciation she receives from the athletes. Seeing their smiles and receiving their hugs makes her feel that she is making a difference in the lives of the athletes. Both volunteers should be commended for their efforts, but Volunteer 1, the intrinsically motivated one, is more likely to sustain her efforts regardless of how the athletes act toward her.

Compare this example to one involving academics. Two third-grade students experience difficulties with reading fluency. Student 1 is intrinsically motivated to read fast. He sees his family reading often and, even without prompting, reads more and more to help establish his own fluency. He may even seek out help from teachers and family to tutor him. Student 2, however, is extrinsically motivated to read fluently. He requires stimuli to celebrate each of his gains. Such stimuli may be verbal praise or even desirable tangible rewards. Like the volunteers, each student is making positive efforts, but one requires less external influence and thus is more likely to continue those efforts.

 A Reflective Moment

How are your students motivated?

_____

_____

Connecting Intrinsic and Extrinsic Motivation

Let's look a little further at the two types of motivation to maximize the success of your students with disabilities. (See the diagram on the next page.) When teachers connect praise to extrinsic tangible or token reinforcers, the student learns what is important and is more likely to build intrinsic motivation. Please note that primary needs are not connected to intrinsic motivation. If a student has basic needs (e.g., food, shelter), then these should *not* be included in a reward and incentive system. (Adapted from Witzel & Mercer, 2003)

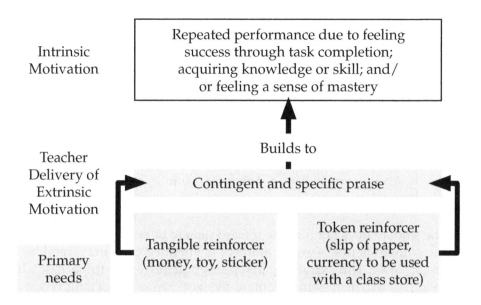

Intrinsic Motivation

Repeated performance due to feeling success through task completion; acquiring knowledge or skill; and/or feeling a sense of mastery

Builds to

Teacher Delivery of Extrinsic Motivation

Contingent and specific praise

Primary needs

Tangible reinforcer (money, toy, sticker)

Token reinforcer (slip of paper, currency to be used with a class store)

Motivating through Extrinsic Means

When a student appears to lack effort, we assume that the student lacks desire. When it comes to lack of engagement in class, again, we assume that the student does not wish to achieve. In such cases, we employ a system of rewards to try to motivate the student. These rewards are attempts at extrinsic reinforcement, where we are setting a student up for success and then rewarding his or her efforts to succeed in hopes that the student repeats similar efforts.

External rewards, despite their intention, do not always equate to positive reinforcement. Reinforcement should be viewed from the student's point of view, not the teacher's (Maag, 2001). Something that is reinforcing leads to repeated or even strengthened performances. Positive reinforcement means a stimuli was added to the environment that caused the recurrence of the desired action. Therefore, when teachers use a reward, they hope to reinforce a desired behavior so that it repeats. When a student appropriately raises his or her hand for the first time to ask a question, the teacher responds with verbal praise commending him or her for the good behavior. If the verbal praise was desired by the student, then he or she will repeat the hand raising. If, however, the student sees the verbal praise as public embarrassment, it is less likely he or she will raise his or her hand in the future. Thus, it is important to recognize that rewards, although potentially powerful, do not always result in positive reinforcement. When the reward is effectively tied to the student's desires, however, the use of the reward will prove powerful.

Since desires can change over time, the use of a single type of reward does not always yield long-term results. For a first grader, a lollipop may be sufficient for effort. However, a tenth grader may in fact be offended by the suggestion of such a reward. See the table that follows for a progression of one student's most desired reinforcer over a twelve-year span.

Candy → Sticker → Token → Money → Grades

If the student does not find the reward item to be worthy of the behavior, then the student is not being reinforced as intended (Schultz, Tremblay, & Hollerman, 2000). Thus, choosing an appropriate reward is important when employing an extrinsic-reinforcement system. More important, however, is how the reward is received.

 Avoid the Roadblock!

Consider rewards from the students' points of view. Some students respond to public praise; others prefer to be rewarded privately.

Unless we plan to use rewards extensively for the same behavior, year after year, the intent should be to help students learn the behavior and repeat it without the presence of the reward. While the receipt of the reward itself is initially important, it is the delivery of the reward and the interaction between the presenter and receiver of the reward that determines the long-term effectiveness. For example, a teacher wants to increase homework completion rates. So, the teacher sets up a chart and provides a sticker for each night a student completes the assigned task. When homework rates rise, the teacher may erroneously conclude that the stickers were the stimuli that improved the behavior. However, the teacher did not consider that when providing stickers, he or she praised individual students for their work and acknowledged their sacrifice of personal time in the evening. For some students, the stickers may not matter, nor may the public announcement of homework completion presented on the wall. What helped these students was verbal praise.

Verbal praise that is contingent upon the completion of desired behavior is considered the most powerful extrinsic reward for long-term effects (Witzel & Mercer, 2003). When a student is rewarded verbally with praise after completing a task or behavior, he or she is eventually able to repeat this praise to herself or himself in order to self-reinforce. Self-talk and self-reinforcement is then able to translate into what may be considered intrinsic motivation.

Following is a list of potential extrinsic rewards. Knowing the importance of contingent verbal praise, it is highly desirable to connect each tangible reward or token to verbal praise that explains what the student did and why he or she is being rewarded.

Extrinsic Examples

- looks of teacher approval
- looks of peer approval
- tokens in an economy system
- money
- desired tangible objects

 ## Avoid the Roadblock!

We must analyze the behavior of our students with learning disabilities, particularly those who appear unmotivated. There are choices you can make as to which area needs focus.

a) If the student appears unmotivated, then employ extrinsic rewards. As behavior improves, gradually fade the use of rewards by implementing more verbal praise and fewer tangible rewards contingent with the behavior.

b) If a student appears motivated but incapable of success, teach the skill or behavior explicitly while mixing extrinsic- and intrinsic-motivation principles to build fidelity.

c) If the student appears motivated and successful with a skill or behavior, then focus efforts on intrinsic motivation.

Barriers

a) If the student does not respond to the verbal praise or after the tangible reward has been removed, then too much emphasis may have been placed on the tangible object. Use verbal praise first without presenting the tangible object. Once you have explained what the student did and why it was so appropriate, then present the tangible object.

b) If the student does not respond to the tangible reward or verbal praise, then the extrinsic system may not be sufficient. Review the use of verbal praise and the student's understanding of the reward system. The tangible reward may not be appropriate. Determine if a token reward system is appropriate for the student so that the student can accept delayed gratification of a tangible reward in exchange for an even more valuable tangible reward. This also helps place more emphasis on verbal praise on the path to the reward.

c) If the student appears confused by the motivation system, then consider simplifying it. There may a mismatch between different classrooms or between home and school that will need to be addressed.

Motivating through Intrinsic Means

Of the two types of motivation, extrinsic is easier to implement; intrinsic is more difficult to build. Because developing intrinsic motivation is so important to building self-efficacy in students, let's look at specific ways to increase intrinsic motivation. Intrinsic motivation comes from within. It's the sense of working toward something simply because we want to or because we see value in the accomplishment. A student may be intrinsically motivated if he or she:

◆ pursues the activity independently
◆ enjoys the activity
◆ wants to work through completion
◆ moves beyond the minimum expectations
◆ is motivated by the task or the learning, not rewards

In schools, we focus much of our time and attention on extrinsic rewards, such as points and prizes, because they are easier to deal with and they do motivate many students, particularly for the short term. Intrinsic motivation, on the other hand, seems to be harder for us, but there are two foundational elements that can help: students are more motivated when they find *value* in what they are doing and when they believe they have a chance for *success*. Teachers can create a learning environment that supports both components. Let's take a look at some strategies that can help.

1. *Value*. Students are more likely to be intrinsically motivated to learn if they value what they are asked to do. Although educators frequently talk about rigor and relevance, value includes relevance and more. Even though it is important for students to see the relevance of learning, sometimes students connect with instruction because they enjoy the class or have a positive relationship with the teacher. There are five ways to add value to your classroom (see page 19).

Ways to Add Value to Instruction

V	Variety	Include a variety of activities, assignments, projects, etc. Have a structure, but don't get caught up in a boring routine.
A	Attractiveness	Integrate elements of movement, curiosity, and originality into your lessons.
L	Locus of control	To address students' need for some control over their circumstances or ownership in the learning, provide opportunities for them to be a part of the learning experience, rather than simply being told what to do.
U	Utility	Students need to see the utility, purpose, or relevance of the lesson. Provide real-life connections.
E	Enjoyment	Students are more motivated when they find pleasure in what they are doing. Although you need to have a classroom with structure and order, that may look different in different classrooms. It is absolutely, positively OK to smile and have fun. Play games, make jokes, and do something different.

Mr. Cook works at an alternative high school for students who have struggled with academics and behavior. Many of the students who come to him have failed repeatedly in school, not because they lack cognitive abilities, but because they have become uninterested in school. In his class, he incorporates socially relevant topics such as dating to teach mathematics problem solving using a spreadsheet and a graph of social trends. He has used technology not just to facilitate learning, but to initiate it. Mr. Cook says that many of his colleagues have struggled working in an alternative school because they thought that they needed to befriend their students to get them to participate and learn. He says that his experience and disproportionately high test scores have come from showing how to apply educational standards and linking them to value for students, which has been severely lacking in these students' lives.

 A Reflective Moment

Which aspect of value would impact your students in a positive manner?

_____

_____

2. *Success.* Students are also motivated when they believe they have a chance to be successful. Too often, we have students who have never been successful in a school setting. Students need to set and achieve goals in order to build a sense of confidence, which leads to a willingness to try something else, which in turn begins a cycle that leads to higher levels of success. As shown in the diagram below, success leads to success, and the achievements of small goals are building blocks to success at larger goals.

Success Cycle

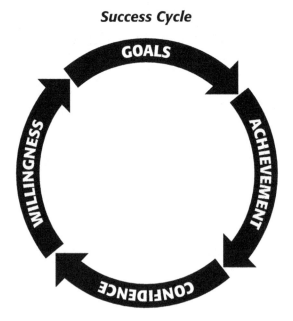

For example, Shane is a struggling student. Shane's teacher knows Shane is capable of the work, but he is unwilling to try. She is frustrated because he does not participate in class and seems uninterested. In a meeting with Shane's mother, the teacher discovered that Shane feels he is never successful in school. Therefore, he doesn't try. The teacher and the mother set small goals for Shane, and the teacher provided extra support to ensure he achieved them. As Shane built confidence in his ability to be successful, he was more willing to try additional tasks. This cycle of setting goals, supporting achievement, feeling confident, then having a willingness to try again makes a clear difference to students. Let's look at a more detailed example of a situation that looks at success differently.

 Avoid the Roadblock!

Chunk assignments into very small steps so students can feel successful in a variety of ways. Also, ask open-ended questions for which there are no wrong answers. Again, creating opportunities for success will help students build confidence in their own learning.

Looking Beneath the Surface

Jessica was in her tenth-grade English class quietly filing her nails at her group's table while Mr. Howard discussed the week's vocabulary. It wasn't the first time she did something other than focus solely on the lesson. Her teacher assumed that her disengagement was linked to her lack of understanding of the lesson. Mr. Howard, like most of us, showed his frustration with Jessica by repeatedly calling on her to answer questions. Without hesitation, she answered each question correctly, with an increasingly annoyed tone to her voice. Eventually Jessica said, "Why are you asking me all of the questions?" Clearly, she understood the lesson but displayed her learning in a manner that Mr. Howard found inappropriate. Mr. Howard instructed the class to complete a short independent assignment and went over to Jessica's desk to ask why she didn't want to pay attention to the lesson. "On the contrary," she replied. "I do pay attention to the lesson. Keeping my hands busy allows me to focus on what you say. Also, don't my nails look great?" Mr. Howard, still annoyed, told her to try to look like she was paying attention. While Mr. Howard wanted a clearer appearance of attention, it is important to recognize Jessica's ability to pay attention to two tasks simultaneously. His definition of appropriate learning behavior was linked to his definition of success. Jessica, however, had been diagnosed with ADHD by her seventh birthday. As such, she struggled for many years with paying attention in school, particularly as classes became more seat-study focused. By the time she was sixteen years old, she had learned how to harness her energy and still keep up in class. Mr. Howard learned through this encounter that some students learn differently. Just because it would be difficult for Mr. Howard, and likely most of the students in the class, to coordinate two different stimuli, Jessica needed to balance the stimuli. As he changed his view of what success looked like and how to assess it, he also learned to support achievement in his students at a more individual level. Jessica was clearly successful, confident, and willing to participate but not in a manner that was familiar to Mr. Howard.

 ## A Reflective Moment

How does Jessica's story apply to your students?

_____

_____

Throughout this book, we'll share examples from our own teaching, as well as words and examples from other teachers we have worked with. You'll also see strategies that are research based and practitioner tested. They are effective, if consistently and persistently applied and adapted to your students' needs.

However, it is important for you to believe that you and your students can be successful and motivated to learn at high levels. Take a few moments and imagine it is the middle of the school year. Your students with special needs are accomplishing more than you thought possible. They are engaged, motivated, and excited to be in your class. How did you create that environment? What did you do to help them be successful? Paint a vision and then accomplish it.

 ## Summary

- Students with disabilities or at-risk concerns have often experienced academic frustration throughout their schooling. For this reason, it is difficult to motivate these learners.
- Extrinsic-motivation techniques involve offering tangible rewards to acknowledge a student's efforts and accomplishments. While this is effective initially, it alone will not make a long-term difference in a student's self-esteem.
- Intrinsic motivation is a student's internal desire to do well or accomplish a task efficiently.
- Students are more motivated when they find _value_ in what they are doing and when they believe they have a chance for _success._
- An educator's charge is to help all students become intrinsically motivated to learn.

3

Setting High Expectations

When we begin to talk about high expectations with teachers, typically we'll hear, "My students don't have high expectations for themselves, and their families don't even have high expectations for them. How do I deal with that?" This is a particular challenge for students who have special needs, since they may not have been held to high expectations in the past. Let's start with how to help students rise to your high expectations and ultimately increase their own.

There are six ways you can put your high expectations into practice.

1. Setting Clear Goals and Expectations
2. Using Positive Language
3. Adopting a "No Excuses" Mentality
4. Establishing a Climate of Success
5. Moving From Weakness to Strength
6. Using Rigorous Questioning Strategies

Setting Clear Goals and Expectations

Eduardo, a tenth-grade English language learner who speaks English as a second language and has learning disabilities, was receiving an intervention on study skills with Brad, who remembers working on a definition from the student's biology textbook.

I asked him to define *photosynthesis*. His first answer was the definition of another word, not even in the same chapter. I looked at him, puzzled, gave him a cue, and asked him again. Ed said that he didn't understand the cue and started to open the book. I placed my hand on the book and tried another cue. Ed looked me in the eye, furrowed his brow, and said, "How am I going to give you the right answer, if I don't know what page it is on?" Curious, I told him the page. He then asked, "At the bottom?" Yes, I replied. Ed went on to recite the definition word for word from the book. We repeated this routine for the next nine words on his vocabulary list. What I concluded was that Ed had developed a visual memory of the book's pages. When he was asked rote questions, he recited answers. This had worked early in his academic career, but, although he was no longer eligible for ELL services, his difficulty with English still interfered with his comprehension of expository text.

From this information, we established new goals for Ed. Teachers realized his brilliance in rote and picture memory, but we set new goals for comprehension of text. Ed realized that he is smart and has a unique skill. Teachers praised him, and he felt good about it. In turn, students responded as well. Instead of treating him as a struggling student, student groups asked Ed to help with studying vocabulary and memorizing diagrams and charts. Ed, in return, asked students to help him understand the text so that he knew what he was memorizing.

Goal setting helped Ed understand his strengths and weaknesses. In addition, this experience helped with his self-esteem because he finally understood why he struggled with certain aspects of school.

A Reflective Moment

How would goal setting positively affect your students?

_____

_____

Knowledge of one's strengths and weaknesses as a learner is necessary to set personal goals, but it is not sufficient for a student's success. Students must also be told what is expected of them in order to gain independence in problem solving at home and the workplace.

Devon

A tier 2 interventionist, Ms. Laurel, was tutoring a student named Devon who had a specific learning disability in math. Devon was in the seventh grade and about fourteen years old, but he appeared to be in his late teens. He read at the second-grade level and was known to be very disruptive in class. In fact, when Ms. Laurel would pick him up for tutoring, the teaching assistant in his classroom would often say, "Good luck with Devon today. We are happy he's leaving so that we can finally work." While it was obvious that Devon distracted other students as much as he distracted himself, the teachers did not do a great job hiding their negative opinions of him. Following such verbal degradation, Devon only acted worse. To add to the difficulty of working with Devon, Ms. Laurel was an attractive new graduate who looked similar in age to Devon. During tutoring, Devon would spend his time flirting and making inappropriate comments rather than working. After all, failing in front of her would be more embarrassing than refusing to work. Ms. Laurel wanted to help Devon academically but needed help with him behaviorally. This is when Ms. Laurel called Brad, an intervention expert from a local university.

> I met Ms. Laurel and Devon in the library. I proceeded to tell Devon my role and expectations of Ms. Laurel during the intervention. Ms. Laurel told Devon her expectations of him. As a team, we agreed on some consequences. If I did not provide Ms. Laurel with effective interventions, then Devon was to contact the principal. I wrote the principal's name. I wrote my office phone number so Devon could contact me if Ms. Laurel was not working diligently to help him. And we wrote that if Devon was not trying to focus during the tutoring, then I would have a meeting with him after school with the principal. However, if everything was going well, not only would his reading improve, but I would buy his favorite book for him. Although Devon looked quite nervous with me there, he asked if I could come back to meet with him and watch the intervention. I stated that I would, but only after two weeks of positive reports from Ms. Laurel. He agreed, and we wrote it in the contract. Oddly enough, he had no major problems with Ms. Laurel for the rest of the six-week intervention. In fact, he wrote me weekly about his progress and continued to ask when I would come back to observe him. I did, often.

Find what motivates a student, and clearly articulate the expectations. In this case, Brad wrote down the expectations in a contract format so that the student understood his demands and potential consequences and rewards. You may not have an extra set of hands like Ms. Laurel did in this situation, but you can use the same principles in your own setting.

Principles

Use predominantly positive, encouraging words.
Provide opportunities for success.
Minimize opportunities for public failure.
Provide a clear, written agreement of expectations.
Use positive follow-up.

In the Devon example, a plan was made to help the student understand what was expected and what he had to do to succeed. For motivation, a reward was set for Devon. In order for the student to understand the responsibilities of all parties, the student's job and the tutor's job were detailed. In this example, the outcome was success. However, in many cases, expectations will need to be revisited and adjusted accordingly.

Choose one student. Use the chart that follows to connect expectations with the student's objective.

Set Goals and Expectations

Goal	Student's Job	Teacher's Job	Reward for Meeting Goal

Using Positive Language

Sometimes students who have been labeled as special needs have heard a lifetime of negative comments regarding their academic efforts. The words we use have a powerful impact on students. Derwin Gray, a former NFL player, says using negative words are like hammering a nail into another person. Even when we say we are sorry, which pulls the nail out, it still leaves a hole. How do we counter the negativity? We begin with our language. When we are asking our students to move to higher levels of learning, they need encouragement. Our words and actions either encourage or discourage.

 Avoid the Roadblock!

The first step to avoiding negative comments is to be aware of them. Pay attention to what you say and how you say it.

It is important for us to respond to appropriate student behavior over inappropriate behavior using a 4:1, or at least a 3:1, ratio in order to increase student engagement and achievement (Witzel, 2007). In the table below, we list examples of encouraging and discouraging responses to student behavior that will help increase appropriate student behavior and/or decrease inappropriate behavior.

Examples of Motivating Language

Encouraging Statements	*Discouraging Statements*
Praise Caroline, you have worked very hard today.	*Rule Reminder* Robert, don't forget about the hand-raising rule.
Praise Your quiz shows you definitely understand the Treaty of Versailles, Laura.	*Verbal Reprimand* You know you should be doing your work right now, Regan.
Noncontingent Attention Gerald, how was your recital last night?	*Correction* It's time you stopped talking and started the warm-up.
Noncontingent Attention Hunter, tell me about your weekend.	*Warning* The next time I tell you to sit down, you will have an after-school detention.
Implementing a Positive System Cate, you earned a star for cleaning your work area.	*Consequences* Lexi! That's enough pushing in line. Go to the office!
Nonverbal Approval Nod, smile, thumbs-up, etc., coupled with eye contact	*Nonverbal Disapproval* Teacher look, attention signal, frown, etc., not necessarily with eye contact

 A Reflective Moment

Think of a negative statement you've heard a teacher say to a student. Now, reword it into a positive statement.

_____

_____

Adopting a "No Excuses" Mentality

Another key part of raising expectations is refusing to allow students to use excuses to avoid learning. For example, many students will "forget" to bring a pencil or paper to class. Often, a teacher will require a student to simply sit in class as a punishment for not being responsible. However, this allows students to forgo learning for the day. Ultimately, we must make a decision about whether to focus on learning or on pencils. In Barbara's classroom, she provided a pencil students could borrow during class. It was a large, pink pencil with feathers, so usually students remembered their pencils the next day. Another alternative is to gather pencils dropped in the hall and use those for students who need them.

Repeated failures and low achievement associated with learning disabilities often lead students to attribute their failures to internal causes and successes to external causes such as luck or ease of the task (Dweck & Elliott, 1983; Settle & Milich, 1999). Attributing success or failure to external sources is referred to as an external locus of control. Students with this attitude develop a learned helplessness over the years, knowing that they will fail, despite even good scores on tests and assignments.

Learned helplessness is a process of conditioning in which student seek help from others even when they have mastered information. See if this example sounds familiar:

A student is asked to solve a direct reading-comprehension problem, but he immediately raises his hand. When the teacher comes over, the student says he needs help. So the teacher reads the paragraph to the student and re-explains the question. The student still doesn't answer the question. Next, the teacher re-explains a regularly used comprehension strategy with the student. Finally, the teacher walks through the strategy and may even solve the problem for the student.

While this teacher's approach sounds justifiable, and maybe even familiar, the teacher is reinforcing the student's learned helplessness. This exchange undermines the student's independent ability to solve the problem. Other behaviors that continue a student's learned helplessness include an increased time of completion, lack of academic perseverance, refusal to initiate an attempt, and general off-task behavior. Thus, once a student has begun a run of learned helplessness, expect to see the behaviors repeatedly. In the scenario above, the student must learn to attend to the teacher's group instruction and attempt to solve problems.

Instead of running to the rescue of students who can succeed without us or even refusing to help such students, it is important to find ways to teach students to gain independence in their problem solving. In other words, find out why the student is behaving in a certain way, and plan a response that best builds academic success and independence. One way to help is to teach students how to learn and succeed without instantly making excuses and asking for help by following these steps.

1. Determine if learned helplessness exists.
2. Explicitly model the preferred academic behavior.
3. Teach the student a strategy for displaying the preferred academic behavior.
4. Provide practice for the strategy.
5. Set a cue to remind the student to initiate the strategy.
6. Allow the student to succeed.
7. Facilitate the student's problem-solving strategy.

Let's use the following scenario to discuss each step.

In a middle school history class, students are working desperately to understand a passage on George Washington. However, Annie hasn't yet begun the assignment. Instead, she rifles through papers and makes grunting sounds of exasperation. The teacher taps Annie's desk as she walks by. Annie rolls her eyes and waves her hand high in a frantic motion like one would make to catch a cab during a rainstorm. The teacher, however, ignores Annie and continues to work with small groups of students. Intermittently, she encourages students who are putting forth effort toward the difficult reading. Annie, irritated that she is being ignored, yells out, "You don't care about me!" (Note: What might look like an insensitive teacher to a passerby is actually a part of an organized effort by school personnel to help Annie overcome learned helplessness. In her IEP, school personnel and Annie's mother agreed to ignore Annie's outbursts when she does not exert effort toward completion of a task).

A few minutes after Annie's outburst, Annie opens her book and begins to work. The teacher goes over to Annie, leans down, and praises Annie for attempting the assignment. She then reminds Annie that she cannot respond to her when she displays such outbursts, let alone when she does not show effort toward the assignment. The teacher also clarifies with Annie the expectation during independent practice. The teacher spends the next five minutes with Annie going over the passage so that she understands the information.

The teacher followed the learned helplessness plan as indicated below.

1. Determine if learned helplessness exists.

The team already determined that Annie's behavior is purposeful and meant to avoid independent work in order to work with the teacher. The behavior occurs in several classes when independent reading is assigned. Although Annie can now read near grade level, she spent several years below grade level and has learned to seek help even if she doesn't need it.

2. Explicitly model the preferred academic behavior.

Teachers have been asked to praise students in class who independently work on assignments. Annie has been asked to watch others' efforts in class to provide a model for what is expected of her.

3. Teach the student a strategy for displaying the preferred academic behavior.

Prior to this class, the special-education and general-education teachers have explained what is expected and how she can gain assistance. The first requirement to receiving help is to show effort for a minimum of three minutes. Then she will be allowed to ask the teacher for help. The number of minutes required for working independently is set to be increased by one minute each week.

4. Provide practice for the strategy.

Last week, Annie practiced the strategy of showing effort for three minutes. It was important that Annie understand what she should be doing as her replacement behavior.

5. Set a cue to remind the student to initiate the strategy.

The cue set by her teachers was a tap on her desk as the teacher walked by. The teacher would not stop by her desk to talk so as to minimize reinforcement for the behavior.

6. Allow the student to succeed.

The teacher did not give in to Annie's demand. Instead, she ignored the inappropriate behavior. When Annie showed three minutes of effort, she immediately went to help Annie for five minutes. The five minutes of help is Annie's incentive for working independently.

7. Facilitate the student's problem-solving strategy.

The teacher followed through with the plan and reminded Annie of the strategy. Overcoming learned helplessness, particularly at this time in her academic career, will be difficult for Annie. The teacher followed the steps appropriately but must remain consistent in her approach in order to help Annie perform more independently. Likewise, Annie's other teachers must remain as diligent.

Establishing a Climate of Success

Establishing a climate of success can counteract learned helplessness by exposing students to role models who faced academic obstacles yet overcame them by setting high expectations for themselves. For example, Charles Schwab didn't let dyslexia stop him. He earned an undergraduate degree in economics (Stanford, '59) and an MBA (Stanford, '61). He once said:

> When I look at the words 'the cat crossed the street,' I have to sound it out to get meaning. Most people get meaning in an automated way. I passed literature classes reading the comic-book versions of such classics as *Moby Dick*. . . . Now that I'm older and focused on investments and economics, I can see some words and concepts clearly. I don't have to go through the slow manipulation in my mind. But if you gave me a book on some subject that I'm not familiar with, it would take me twice as long to read it as anybody else. Even then, I'd have a tough time answering questions on what I've read. I don't read books; I listen to books on tape. Thank goodness for all the new communications devices such as point and click.

This story and the ones of other celebrities describe people who overcame difficulty in a specific area of academics. To achieve despite the area of concern, they found their niches by achieving highly in other areas. If we examine ourselves, we find that we all have to "hide" some weaknesses with strengths in other areas.

What You Can Do

- Fill your room with examples of positive role models.
- Post pictures, read stories, and bring in former students.
- Contact community leaders who have disabilities or overcame something to succeed.
- Give short assignments to investigate famous people who have succeeded.

As a starting point, the table below lists famous people with learning disabilities.

William Hewlett, cofounder, Hewlett Packard
Ted Turner, president, Turner Broadcasting System
Walt Disney, film producer
Agatha Christie, writer
Tommy Hilfiger, clothing designer
Erin Brockovich, investigator
Cher, singer
Nolan Ryan, baseball pitcher
Magic Johnson, basketball player
Orlando Bloom, actor
Tom Cruise, actor
Whoopi Goldberg, actor
Keira Knightley, actor

 A Reflective Moment

What is one thing you will do to promote positive role models in your classroom?

_____

_____

Moving from Weakness to Strength

We need not only to help students understand their weaknesses and recognize them as things that need attention in order to improve, but we must also help students recognize, and in some cases find, their strengths. Next, we need to show students how they can use these strengths as gifts to create their own niches. For example, if a student is good with his or her hands and problem solving, that strength might be turned into an excellent career in a technical service profession. If a student has a good memory and a charming personality, perhaps marketing has potential. No matter what the student chooses, presenting potentials and goals may help students find new energy to work toward those goals. This can be the difference between achievers and nonachievers in our classrooms.

Achievers	Nonachievers
1. Strengths are understood. (metacognition)	Strengths are not understood.
a) Those strengths are valuable to a group of people. (extrinsic motivation)	The person's strengths do not have immediate value to anyone or anything.
b) Those strengths are of interest to the person. (intrinsic motivation)	The person's strengths do not interest the person.
c) The person recognizes the need to continuously improve upon the strength. (attitude)	The person thinks that he or she is the only person with such a strength or gift.
2. Goals are set and owned by the person. (self-determinism)	The person will not set a personal goal nor act upon a plan set by another.
a) The person has a passion to achieve. (energy)	The person isn't interested in achievement or success.
b) A path toward success is articulated. (plan)	How to achieve is not understood.
c) The goal can be achieved with the right attitude and a plan.	The goal and short-term objectives are not seen as attainable.
3. Weaknesses are understood. (metacognition)	Weaknesses are not understood.
a) The person owns the weakness and wants to improve and learn. (awareness)	The person does not recognize his or her possible weaknesses.
b) The person is teachable. (attitude)	The person does not desire to learn how to improve.

Understanding the differences between students who are achievers and nonachievers helps us better scaffold learning so that nonachievers become achievers. One of the ways we can work more effectively with nonachievers is through our questioning.

Using Rigorous Questioning Strategies

In establishing high expectations for our students with disabilities, we must examine the questions we ask them. If we consistently ask them low-level fact/recall questions, it can send a message that this is all we think they are capable of answering. There are many models for organizing higher levels of questions, but we will look at three: the new Bloom's Taxonomy, Costa's House of Questions, and Quality QUESTIONS. Each takes a slightly different approach and can be adapted for your precise purposes.

New Bloom's Taxonomy

The original Bloom's Taxonomy of Educational Objectives, released in 1956, was designed to help teachers write objectives and create tests to address a variety of levels of understanding. In 2001, a group of researchers revised the original taxonomy to include a more rigorous progression (see page 35).

By crossing the knowledge row with the process column, you can plan objectives, activities, and assessments that allow students to learn different types of knowledge using a variety of processes. The widely used revised taxonomy is a complex but useful method for addressing all levels of questioning.

Bloom's Taxonomy of Educational Objectives

The Knowledge Dimension	The Cognitive Process Dimension					
	Remember	Understand	Apply	Analyze	Evaluate	Create
Factual	recognize	interpret	execute	organize	critique	construct
Conceptual	recall	classify	employ	disseminate	assess	produce
Procedural	define	summarize	implement	investigate	review	conceptualize
Metacognitive	distinguish	infer	perform	differentiate	judge	generate

Source: Anderson/Krathwohl/Airasian/Cruikshank/Mayer/Pintrich/Raths/Wittrock, *A Taxonomy for Learning, Teaching, and Assessing: A Revision of Bloom's Taxonomy of Educational Objectives* Abridged Edition, 1st © 2001. Printed and electronically reproduced by permission of Pearson Education, Inc., Upper Saddle River, New Jersey. Adapted by permission of the publisher.
Note: The verbs are interchangeable among the columns. For example, one could recognize factual, conceptual, procedural, and/or metacognitive information.

Costa's House of Questions

Costa and Kallick authors of *Learning and Leading with Habits of Mind*, provide a different model. It is a three-level, user-friendly, practical "story house" that describes the levels of questioning (see the figure below). We've observed this model used in several AVID (Advancement Via Individual Determination, www.avid.org) classrooms, and it is effective for both students and teachers.

Level One	Level Two	Level Three
Defining, identifying, naming, reciting, describing, listing, observing, scanning	Analyzing, contrasting, inferring, comparing, grouping, sequencing, synthesizing	Applying a principle, hypothesizing, judging, evaluating, imagining, predicting, speculating

Quality QUESTIONS

Finally, no matter which model of questioning you use, it's important to reflect on the quality of questions you create. Following are nine reminders, around an acrostic of QUESTIONS, to help guide your development of questions during lessons.

Quality. First, questions should be of high quality. That means each question should be relevant and understandable to your students. Recently, Barbara was in a classroom in which the students were struggling to answer the questions. The teacher assumed they didn't know the content. That wasn't true; they didn't know what he was asking. The questions were very broad and somewhat related to the lesson, but even she wasn't sure what he was asking. The next day, he reviewed the material with a set of clear, focused questions, and the students were more successful.

Understanding. Good questioning serves as a road map for students; it guides them to higher levels of understanding. Barbara Liebhaber of Moravian College in Chicago models a discussion lesson for prospective teachers using guided questioning. Later in the semester, as her students are creating their own lessons, she explains:

They discover that asking questions helps their lessons because then the learner owns the information, is more connected to it, finds it relevant, and is therefore motivated to learn. When I ask them how they discovered this, they refer back to the lesson that I did on defining the adolescent and see that I was, in fact, modeling that lesson for them. It takes them a while to discover this, but when they do we all get a laugh out of it. They didn't know, at the time, that I was modeling and making the point about questioning students. They thought they were just talking about being teenagers again. In this way, learning is taking place in an active way that is relevant and meaningful for the students. The point is made by modeling and questioning, not telling anything. And it is made in a stronger way than if I told them to ask questions of their students because it is a good way to teach.

Encourage Multiple Responses. As you create questions for your students, remember to build in questions that are open-ended, those that have more than one answer. Although it is important to ask questions about facts and details that have only one answer, higher-level questions generally have several possible responses. These "how" and "why" questions will prepare students for life after school.

Spark New Questions. Similarly, good questioning should encourage more questions. In a lesson about food groups, for example, questions about healthy eating might lead your students to ask about the food served for lunch in the cafeteria and the sale of soft drinks in school vending machines. This could lead to a discussion about the school's role in promoting healthy eating. That's exactly what you want to happen. If your students begin to make those connections, it is an indication that they are learning.

Thought Provoking. In addition to prompting new questions, good questioning should provoke students to think. This is more than a regurgitation of facts; it means that students are actively thinking about their learning—what it means, how they are processing the information, and how it connects to their lives. In her book *Yellow Brick Roads: Shared and Guided Paths to Independent Reading 4–12*, Janet Allen provides categories of questions that allow students to process the content and their own learning. We've adapted it into a bookmark that students can use as they read to prompt questioning. (See the next page.) You can do the same thing using categories that are appropriate for your content area.

Questioning Bookmark

How would I feel or react?

Does this make sense?
Why did I think that?

How would my friends react to
this? Would my friends do this?

How does this compare to . . . ?
What would I change?

How does the picture help me?
What does the subheading mean?

Individualized. We should also customize questioning techniques for different students. One of Barbara's less confident students, Ronnie, was reluctant to volunteer to answer questions. As Barbara explains, "I would ask him a question that I knew he could answer. Sometimes it was an opinion question rather than a literal, fact-based one. But I wanted to make sure he could be successful so that he would be more confident later."

It's also important to provide different ways for students to answer questions. For example, Cynthia Crump uses signaling with her math students. As she explains, "When [my students] are all working individually on a problem, they signal me with their fingers what the answer is. I can stand in the front of the room and acknowledge whether the answer is correct or not very quickly. It beats trying to run around the room and check answers. Plus, the students are very creative in the ways that they present their answers. There is not a 'correct' way. [When] they give me the tens and then the ones for example, sometimes they form the numbers with their fingers, and sometimes they give me the digits, etc. They love it because it moves quickly and allows the slower students to use the time that they need before someone gives the answer out loud. Plus they have immediate feedback. Faster students simply go on to the next problem." Her system allows each student to thrive.

Ownership Shifted to Students. Kathy Bumgardner, a reading specialist for the Gaston County Schools in North Carolina, introduced Barbara to the Question Matrix (Weiderhold, 1995). (See the matrix on the next page.) This grid crosses basic questions (*who, what, when, where, why,* and *how*) with verbs (*is, did, can, would, will,* and *might*) to create a matrix that addresses all levels of questioning. If you divide the grid into four quadrants, you'll notice the upper left addresses basic questions; the closer you get to the bottom right, the higher the level of questioning. Copy the grid on bright colors of card stock, cut the squares apart, and put a complete set in a plastic bag. After students have read a portion of text or when you are reviewing for a test, put them into small groups and give each group a bag of cards. Each student draws a card and has to finish the question. For example, if I draw the question frame "How would . . . ?" I might ask, "How would you react if you lived in a country that faced a famine?" Then, the rest of the group must answer the question. Barbara has done this activity with hundreds of teachers in her workshops, and you can use these questions with almost any topic. It's interactive and engaging, but most importantly, it shifts ownership of the activity to students. They are responsible for creating their own questions, and that requires them to understand the material at a high level.

Question Matrix

What Is	When Is	Where Is	Which Is	Who Is	Why Is	How Is
What Did	When Did	Where Did	Which Did	Who Did	Why Did	How Did
What Can	When Can	Where Can	Which Can	Who Can	Why Can	How Can
What Would	When Would	Where Would	Which Would	Who Would	Why Would	How Would
What Will	When Will	Where Will	Which Will	Who Will	Why Will	How Will
What Might	When Might	Where Might	Which Might	Who Might	Why Might	How Might

Source: Wiederhold (1995).

Narrow and Broad. Earlier, we mentioned the importance of using open-ended, high-level questioning. There is a balance. Because knowledge is based on facts, you want to include questions that are narrow and focused on a single answer. However, you also want to include questions that are broader and are generally considered application questions. Bloom's Taxonomy is a helpful planning tool.

Sample Questions for an Elementary Science Lesson on the Inner Planets Using Bloom's Taxonomy

Remembering: Understanding:
What is the closest planet to the sun?
Why is a year on Mercury much shorter than a year on Earth?
How old would you be if you lived on Mars?

Applying: Analyzing: Evaluating:
Why is it possible to live on Earth but not on Mars?
Do you think we should be spending so much time and effort on space exploration?

Creating:
Create a colony on the moon. Include the elements needed to survive.

Success Building. Each of the previous recommendations supports the critical purpose of good questioning, leading your students to successful learning. Questions are not simply part of your lesson; they are the key to unlocking understanding for students. Too often, we ask students to read or listen to something and then assume that they know it. Real understanding is more than that, and it doesn't happen through osmosis. It happens when students interact with knowledge in a way that enables them to connect it to what they already know and to their own experiences. Good questioning helps them with that process and ensures their success.

Successful Student Learning

Remember, the goal of all questioning is successful student learning. As you create and/or adapt lessons to incorporate more rigorous opportunities for learning, you may want to consider the questions that are embedded within your instruction. Barbara recently talked with a teacher who was using high standards and complex activities, but she asked her students basic recall or memory-based questions to assess their understanding. That defeats the purpose. High-level questioning, which includes probing or extending questions, is an integral part of a rigorous classroom.

 Avoid the Roadblock!

"Never do I allow students to give up or settle for mediocrity. . . . I always press them to go to the next level—to challenge themselves and prove anyone wrong who dares to think they cannot succeed!"

—Kawana Dobbins, special-education assessor in Guam (Department of Defense schools)

 Summary

+ Often, either consciously or subconsciously, teachers lower their expectations for students with disabilities when they should be communicating high expectations to increase student motivation and success.
+ By providing clear expectations and using positive language, teachers can help students learn to set attainable, yet challenging, goals for themselves.

4

Providing Support

In order for students to learn at high levels, we must provide the appropriate support. There are six specific types of support that are helpful.

1. Scaffolding
2. Modeling
3. Thinking Aloud
4. Providing Guides and Graphic Organizers
5. Using Concrete-Representational-Abstract
6. Teaching Community Skills
7. Applying Modifications and Accommodations

Scaffolding

Rooted in Bruner (1960) and Vygotsky (1978), the purpose of scaffolding is to help students learn new information. Like scaffolding on a building, instructional scaffolding involves applying supports and strategies to help students achieve. As the student succeeds, scaffolds are faded with the goal of independent student success.

There are several types of scaffolds, from providing examples to guided notes to graphic organizers. For example, a student who is struggling with multiplication tables may be allowed to use a multiplication chart to look for the facts. As the student masters certain facts, those numbers are erased or covered so that they no longer show on the chart. Thus, the only facts that remain are the ones the student has yet to memorize. A similar approach can be used with behavior checklists to help a student learn to raise his or her hand or a peer coach to help check vocabulary and spelling.

When introducing scaffolds, connect concepts across your curriculum and start with problems that students can solve. The scaffold itself, while important, is typically ineffective if the student is not shown how to use it and if it is not faded as the student shows improvement.

Examples of Scaffolding

Cue cards
Hints and prompting questions
Question starters
Visuals
Stories and examples

Applying Lessons Learned: A Sample Activity

Mary Sanford teaches special-needs students at Sullivan Middle School. There are four key elements to her scaffolded instruction: chunking instruction, cycles of repeated instruction, modeling for support, and use of visuals.

Teaching Characterization to Special-Needs Students Who Are Second-Language Learners
My students lacked the vocabulary (for example, *coldhearted*, *persistent*, *generous*) necessary to describe characters and had limited exposure to working with characterization. I needed to break down the task and introduce it one piece at a time. I approached the task knowing I needed to model for my students. I modeled my strategies, I modeled my thinking, I modeled what I wanted them to do, and then we practiced, practiced, practiced.

Students were given a list of traits, both positive and negative. After reading the list together, students found words they would use to describe themselves. I modeled by describing things I do, and the students had to find the trait from the list that went with my behavior, such as, 'I believed him when he said the dog ate his homework'—gullible. When they became comfortable using the list, they were asked to write down three of their own character traits and support why they chose each trait with an example of how they behave.

As we read several short stories, we discussed main characters and found words to describe them. We wrote paragraphs describing these characters using the new words we had learned. Using a Venn diagram, we compared two characters from the same story.

We were then ready to create our own characters. I modeled this first by creating my own character and answering a series of guiding questions on the overhead for them to see. We discussed how the answers had to blend together for the character to be believable. Each character had to have a name and a problem he or she was dealing with. With this information complete, the skeleton "Fleshing Out The Character" from Janet Allen (see below) was filled in with what the character would do, say, plan, think, and feel. We finished the project by illustrating the character. This hands-on component engaged every student. They could draw the character, but most chose to cut out body parts from magazines and put the parts together. This was fun, and students had to know their characters in order to put together pictures that matched their characters' descriptions and lifestyles. We put this completed work in a safe place and will return to it later in the year when we are ready to write short stories.

Flesh It Out

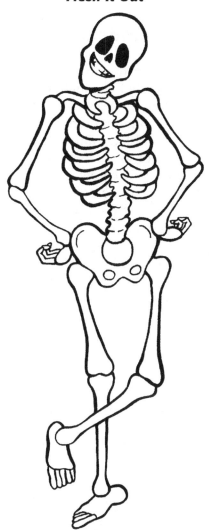

Skeleton drawing © 2008 Mike Sudduth &
Carlee Lingerfelt. Used with permission.

Mary also used picture books such as *Amazing Grace* and *I Wanna Iguana* to reinforce character traits. To extend learning, students read comic strips and had to read between the lines to interpret the cartoons.

As you read the description of Mary's unit, you see how she plans a series of lessons in which she chunks her instruction into small, manageable bites. She then uses an ongoing cycle of providing instruction that teaches the same concept but in different ways. Too often, we make the mistake of teaching the concept multiple times, but simply repeating the same lesson over and over isn't effective. She provides scaffolding through modeling and guided instruction and incorporates visual reinforcement throughout the lesson. The result? Her students with special needs are successful, confident learners.

Modeling

Not every student comes to school ready to learn. This is not merely a kindergarten concern, but one that expands across grade levels. Students need models to know what they should strive to do and why they are doing it. Even when we don't plan to model what to do and why, students are observing, asking questions, and later mimicking our behavior and habits of learning. From social behavior to reading with inflection to solving word problems, children use adults to learn how to do things. When we don't provide clear models, children even use one another.

There are key ways you can model for your students. First, you can model expected instructional behaviors. For example, if your students are not paying attention, you can teach your students the SLANT model (Ellis, 1991). By learning the SLANT model, students learn how to appear like they are paying attention and, in turn, may improve their actual academic engagement.

SLANT

S it up.
L ean forward.
A ct attentive, using varied facial expressions.
N ame the big ideas.
T rack the speaker, maintaining intermittent eye contact.

Next, you can model expected assignments. For example, if students are to write a paragraph or an extended response, it's critical that they see samples of what you expect. We've found that showing two or three samples of good work helps students more effectively complete the assignment.

Finally, consider that modeling follows a three-step process: "I do it, we do it, you do it." First, you complete the task, process, or assignment as a model for the students. Second, you and the students work together through the process. After students are successful, then they try it independently.

 A Reflective Moment

How do you currently provide scaffolding and modeling for your students? How can you provide additional scaffolding and modeling?

_____

_____

Thinking Aloud

A useful modeling technique is a think-aloud. A think-aloud is a teacher verbalizing his or her thoughts and reasoning when solving a problem, making sense of text, or completing a task. In math, it may be explaining stepwise reasoning. (See the example below.) In reading, it may be stopping during reading and checking comprehension, asking questions, or making predictions.

Math example:

$$\begin{array}{r} 63 \\ -\ 27 \\ \hline \end{array}$$
Teacher: In this problem, I am subtracting 27 from 63. This means that I have positive 63 and must go to the left on a number line 27.

$$\begin{array}{rr} +60 & +3 \\ -20 & -7 \\ \hline \end{array}$$
Teacher: I want to use place value to make better sense of how to do this efficiently. So, I am going to separate the minuend, 63, and the subtrahend, –27, each by their place value and line them up accordingly.

$$\begin{array}{rr} +60 & +3 \\ -20 & -7 \\ \hline +40 & -4 \end{array}$$
Teacher: I will solve the tens place first and then the ones. 6 tens minus 2 tens is 4 tens. 3 minus 7 on a number line is –4.

$$\begin{array}{rr} +60 & +3 \\ -20 & -7 \\ \hline +40 & -4 \\ \hline \end{array}$$
Teacher: I am left with the two differences per place value, +40 and –4. 40 – 4 is 36. The answer is 36. Looking back over the question of 63 – 27, the answer of 36 makes sense.

+36

A think-aloud is one of the most positive scaffolding strategies you can use. Struggling students, especially those with learning disabilities, need to understand the thought process used in solving problems or reading a text. Without a think-aloud, it's simply a code they don't know how to unlock.

 Avoid the Roadblock!

It's important to consider think-alouds from the students' perspectives. Sometimes, it's easy to generalize or skip a few steps because we know the process so well. Remember, your students are beginners.

Providing Guides and Graphic Organizers

It is crucial for students to develop mental images to better organize what they have learned. Using visuals in class is important in helping students create mental images, which makes replication and application of new material more effective. In elementary mathematics, teachers use the number line to show counting and operations or graphic organizers to show different word-problem types and how to solve them. In high school math, T-charts (see below) are frequently used to help plan graphing. They are also used in classes across the curriculum for comparison and contrast.

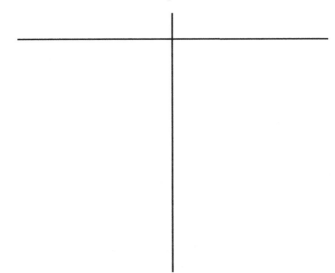

In literacy across the curriculum, different types of graphic organizers are used to help with reading and writing both narrative and expository text.

In the example on the next page, a teacher uses a graphic organizer to help prepare students to write a short paper about clouds. Graphic organizers like this one require students to plan their thoughts before they hurry to put ink on their paper.

Weather Graphic Organizer

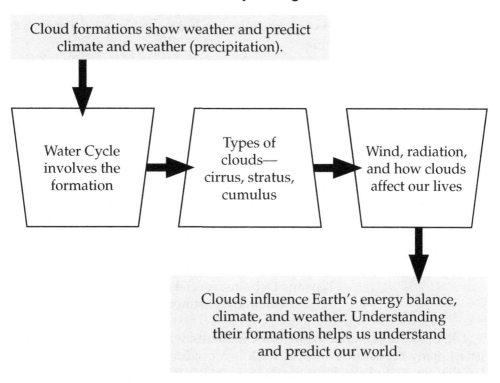

Cloud formations show weather and predict climate and weather (precipitation).

Water Cycle involves the formation

Types of clouds— cirrus, stratus, cumulus

Wind, radiation, and how clouds affect our lives

Clouds influence Earth's energy balance, climate, and weather. Understanding their formations helps us understand and predict our world.

Similarly, graphic organizers can be used to make meaning of text. When reading a complex article about the advantages and disadvantages of both the Confederate and Union armies during the Civil War, a teacher can help students extract facts from expository text with the use of a graphic organizer.

Advantages for the Union Army	*Disadvantages for the Union Army*
◆ Monetary support from England ◆ Constant supply of uniforms, food, weapons, and mercenaries from European countries	◆ Not accustomed to guerilla warfare ◆ Didn't know the backwoods of the South
Advantages for the Confederate Army	*Disadvantages for the Confederate Army*
◆ Fighting on home turf ◆ Accustomed to living off the land and surviving in the woods	◆ Lack of money and resources since trade with Europe was cut off ◆ Unfamiliar with naval warfare; had fewer ships

Whether using visuals to help make meaning of text, organize thoughts before writing, or provide context for a lesson, they should be utilized throughout every lesson to stimulate learning and boost comprehension as a means of supporting learning.

Using Concrete-Representational-Abstract

"Given that I am a special-education teacher, it is my duty to keep up-to-date on research-based strategies to help students learn academic content. I think about and introduce various methods for solving problems through the use of Concrete-Representational-Abstract (CRA) models. Students are able to choose which method works for them, and then we move to the next level. I, along with the regular-education teachers I work with, offer various ways for students to be tutored and tested for the content."

—Kawana Dobbins, special-education assessor in
Guam (Department of Defense schools)

CRA has shown effectiveness for students with and without disabilities in many academic contexts. CRA is a graduated sequence of instruction that takes students from hands-on learning to pictorial representations to abstract reasoning. To design CRA instruction, each level of instruction matches the others so that students can more seamlessly go from level to level. For example, you expect students to understand three steps to solve single-variable math equations. With this in mind, concrete, pictorial representation, and abstract learning must all have the same three steps. Consistent throughout each level is verbal reasoning (see think-alouds) that explains the mathematics behind each step. Students are taken from one level of learning to the next until they are fluent at the abstract level.

Let's look at an example of how CRA was used to help one senior in high school. Courtney felt she was worthless and incapable of learning mathematics. At the end of her twelfth-grade year she finished Algebra 1 with a 59 percent average. The teacher explained to her that she should not be held back from graduation for her lack of math understanding. The injustice to her education was one concern; the fact that she had to complete another math class to graduate was a greater concern to Courtney. She enrolled in an Algebra 2 adult-education summer course. She was petrified, and after the first week she was in panic about how to pass this course. She called her high school counselor, who called Brad, wondering how he could help. Brad worked some explicit CRA methods in basic algebra. She had completed this information a long time back, but she never understood it fully. By covering the old methods and learning the concepts, she was immediately able to generalize the knowledge to her Algebra 2 course. Her summer teacher was so impressed with her gains and so excited by her discoveries that he asked her on several occasions to explain her knowledge to the class. She passed Algebra 2 and graduated that summer, thanks to the power of creative and effective education.

A Reflective Moment

What did you learn from Courtney's story? How will that help you in your classroom?

_____

_____

Teaching Community Skills

In providing support for our students, we must remember to teach them how to support one another. One excellent school district we work with uses a four-step process during the instruction of new skills. They follow a Me-We-Two-You process of learning. This means that for the "Me", the teacher models using a think-aloud first. Second, "We", the teacher uses guided practice by dialoguing with students to help them learn by verbalizing the steps similar to those in the think-aloud. In the "Two" stage, the students verbalize their reasoning, understanding, and thought processes in small groups or with a partner as they collaborate to solve problems. Finally, the students work independently, the "You" stage. The Interactive Reading Guide (see the next page) is an excellent tool to help with this process.

Interactive Reading Guide

Write Time for Kids
"Earth's Baffling Climate Machine"

Individually—Quickly write down your thoughts on Earth's climate. Do you think it's getting warmer? Why or why not? Do you think humans need to change their ways?

Together—Share your thoughts.

Together—Read the expository piece on the Earth's rising climate.

Partner A—Phil Jones makes an interesting statement. When asked about the cause of the warming climate, he says that it is not "a simple case of either-or." What do you think he means by that? Is there another phrase you would use to describe his perspective?

Partner B—Tom Wigley makes a statement about the visibility of rising sea levels. What effect will that have on your everyday life? What will happen if the sea levels rise quickly? Whose lives will be affected the most? How might this affect the creatures of the sea?

Individually—Make connections with what you have just read to information on global warming that the media has put out recently. Use the Internet or newspapers to find updated information.

Together—Discuss what you found. Is the situation getting worse or better? Create a visual that explains your perspective.

Together—Brainstorm ideas on how humanity can attempt to combat global warming.

Individually—Write a letter to the editor of your local paper or write a blog entry about your opinion.

Think-Pair-Share is another effective strategy for students to use. After the teacher asks a question, students are given time to think or reflect on their answers. Next, they turn to a partner and share their answers. Finally, they can share with the entire group. One way to make this strategy more rigorous is to ask students to share their partner's answer with the large group. This requires students to listen at a higher level and to actually reteach their partner's answer.

Finally, working together in small groups is an essential life skill. Whether you group students in sets of three, four, or five, it's important that each student understand his or her task as well as his or her specific role in the group. It is helpful to teach students the practices of effective group work, model those practices, and provide a clear rubric. (See the example on the next page.)

Student Cooperative Learning Rubric

	You're a Team Player **3**	You're Working on It... **2**	You're the Lone Ranger **1**	Total for Each Category
G Group Dedication	I listened respectfully to my teammates' ideas and offered suggestions that helped my group.	I did listen to ideas, but I didn't give suggestions.	I was distracted and more interested in the other groups than my group.	Group Dedication I circled number 3 2 1
R Responsibility	I eagerly accepted responsibility with my group and tried to do my part to help everyone in my group.	I accepted responsibility within my group without arguing.	I quarreled and did not accept roles given by my group.	Responsibility I circled number 3 2 1
O Open Communication	I listened to others' ideas and tried to solve conflicts peacefully.	I listened to others' ideas, but did not try to solve conflicts.	I was controlling and argumentative to my group.	Open Communication I circled number 3 2 1
U Use of Work Time	I was involved and engaged; I encouraged my group the entire time we were working.	I tried my best the entire time we were working.	I was not involved and did not offer any suggestions for the good of the group.	Use of Work Time I circled number 3 2 1
P Participation	I was a team member. I offered ideas, suggestions, and help for my group.	I participated in the project, but did not offer to help anyone.	I did not participate because I was not interested.	Participation I circled number 3 2 1
				Total _____

How do your students currently work in groups? What strategies might you use to improve their collaborative skills?

_____

_____

Applying Modifications and Accommodations

It is erroneous to use the term *modification* interchangeably with the term *accommodation* (Hollenbeck, Tindal, & Almond, 1998), since they are actually very different in concept and purpose. A modification is a change in the content of curricular standards, whereas an accommodation is a tool to help one reach the standard.

Modifications

Modifications are changes to what a student is expected to learn. In other words, the standard or concept is changed from general-education expectations. Content modifications likely change what the test measures (McDonnell, McLaughlin, & Morison, 1997). Modifications, for example, may include deleting certain items that are inappropriate for an examinee or making constructed-response questions into multiple-choice questions. These types of modifications are presumed to change the nature of what is being tested. For standardized assessments, statewide or Common Core related, safeguards exist to secure that the construct of the question will not be altered or modified. Thus, the more modifications given to students during their learning, the less likely that they will be prepared for an unmodified assessment.

For example, a student named Bobby has poor fine-motor skills, which slow down his handwriting. As a response, the IEP team set a homework adaptation that requires him to complete only 75 percent of the homework. Other students are required to complete 100 percent. This is a modification if Bobby has to complete only the first three-quarters of the questions, truncating the more complex ones at the end of the assignment. As a modification, Bobby will not have to complete problems that he may see on the next assessment. Thus, one must question Bobby's preparation. However, if the teacher purposely assigns three-quarters of the questions so that each type of problem must be solved, then it should not be considered a modification. Each question type that Bobby may see on the assessment will be included in his homework. In this case, the reduced number of questions is an accommodation because Bobby is still required to answer questions from each curricular objective, just not as many as other students.

Accommodations

Accommodations are changes that can be made to the way students with disabilities are instructed and assessed. The changes can be made to instructional methods and materials, assignments and assessments, learning environments, time demands and schedules, and communication systems.

In one case, a student, Yvette, who evidences difficulties with long division, may actually have difficulty with multiplication facts. By providing support with multiplication facts through additional interventions and/or multiplication accommodations, a teacher may improve Yvette's belief in her knowledge of mathematics. Subsequently, this minor success in mathematics can be applied to solving long division problems. Thus, it is important to determine where a student is struggling and why. Using that information, you can develop a plan for remediating the area of weakness and supporting the student's learning. Below is a sample analysis of Yvette's difficulty with a math skill.

Yvette's Task Analysis: Struggling in Long Division

Potential Area(s) of Difficulty	Multiplication facts	Paper organization and steps	General understanding of division
Potential Accommodations to Support Her	Use of multiplication tables or calculator	Breaking down task into more manageable chunks and checking in after each	Reteaching concept using manipulatives

Your state and/or school district may have an approved list of accommodations and modifications, but here are a few of the most common ones.

Potential Accommodations	*Potential Modifications*
Extra wait time	Altered grading procedures
Procedures clarification	Alternate (but related) standard
Minimizing classroom distractions	during lesson
Homework reminders and	Different reading assignments
planners	Different questions
Weekly progress report and home	Alternate assessment content and/
checks	or expectations
Increased one-to-one assistance	Elimination of parts of assign-
Classroom signals for attention	ments if they remove a
Visual organizer	standard
Scribe or note taker	Calculator during math-fluency
Guided notes	assignment
Shortened assignments (if all learn-	Altered grading procedures
ing objectives are still covered)	Different reading assignments if
Breaking lengthy assignments	reading is being assessed
into smaller, more manageable	
pieces with intermediate	
deadlines	
Increased frequency of praise and	
encouragement	
Extended time on tests	

Keep in mind that using accommodations does not mean that you are lessening rigor. A key part of the definition of rigor is that appropriate scaffolding is used so that students can be successful at higher levels of learning. Accommodations are simply another type of scaffolding.

 Avoid the Roadblock!

Remember the differences between accommodations and modifications. Be sure to check the IEP of each student to see what is required, and then implement appropriately. Also, remember that the IEP is the floor, not the ceiling, and therefore you can use additional strategies as appropriate.

 Summary

♦ Providing intentional, purposeful support to students with learning disabilities can help them succeed in a rigorous environment.
♦ The use of scaffolding, modeling, and CRA provide concrete examples of what learning looks like.
♦ Accommodations and modifications may need to be used to maximize the success of your special-education students.

5

Demonstration of Student Learning (Assessment)

Students can demonstrate learning at high levels in many different ways. Scott Bauserman, a teacher at Decatur Central High School in Indiana, asks his students to choose a topic from the social studies unit and design a game. The finished product must teach about the topic, use appropriate vocabulary and processes, and be fun to play. As he explains,

> Students have to construct the game, the box, provide pieces and a board, and write the rules. I received a wide variety. One game I will always remember was about how a bill gets passed into law. We spent time [in class] talking about all the points where a bill in Congress or the state General Assembly could be killed, pigeonholed, or defeated. The student took a box the size of a cereal box, set up a pathway with appropriate steps along the way, constructed question/answer cards, and found an array of tokens for game pieces. If a player answered a question correctly, he or she would roll a die and move along the path to passage. But the student had cut trapdoors at the points where a bill could be killed, and if a player landed on a trapdoor/bill stopper, the player to the right could pull a string, making that player's token disappear from the board. The player would have to start over. Not a bad game from a student who has fetal alcohol syndrome and is still struggling to pass his classes.

Scott's example shows the benefit of varying assessments for students with special needs. The way in which you assess students can have a tremendous impact on learning. Let's take a look at creative ways to think about assessment so that your students with special needs have full opportunity to show their growth and knowledge.

Formative Assessment

There are many ways you can gather data and use it to design instruction. We will not take the time to fully investigate formative assessment; that would take an entire book. For our purposes, simply recognize that the instructional strategies described throughout this book are excellent ways to determine if your students are learning.

Formative assessment is a three-step process: observe your students' performance; evaluate what, how, and why they are performing as they do; and adjust your instruction accordingly.

Help Students GROW

G—Gauge where your students are.
R—Recognize their strengths and weaknesses.
O—One step at a time, provide instruction to help them grow.
W—Watch them rise to higher levels.

A Reflective Moment

How do you use assessment to help students grow?

_____

_____

Student performance scores through formative assessment are used to help reformat programs, but they are mainly used to monitor student performance and make small adjustments. The following are three facets of formative assessment.

Diagnostic Assessment
Progress Monitoring
Celebrating Progress

Diagnostic Assessment

Diagnostic assessment is designed to learn the reason why a student is answering questions and solving problems a certain way so that you can help him or her grow. When a student repeats the same error in a set of similar questions, it is called an error pattern. If a teacher can learn why a student is getting incorrect answers, then the teacher can reteach the student directly based on that error. When a teacher doesn't understand why, he or she must reteach the entire process. Reteaching the entire process is inefficient and often ineffective. With experience, the teacher can plan lessons based on previous students' understandings, presenting nonexamples, and warning of typical error patterns. On a positive note, when a teacher learns what and why students understand a concept, he or she knows to repeat certain educational steps. Thus, assessment should be in-depth and frequent so that we catch students' errors early, before they are repeated and learned.

 ## A Reflective Moment

What types of diagnostic assessment do you use in your classroom?

_____

_____

Progress Monitoring

Progress monitoring, a type of formative assessment, is a scientifically based practice that is used to assess students' academic performance and evaluate the effectiveness of instruction. Progress monitoring can be implemented with individual students or an entire class.

To implement progress monitoring, a student's current levels of performance are determined and goals are identified for learning via diagnostic assessments that will take place over time. The use of progress monitoring is connected to curriculum-based measurement, which is used to provide teachers with information on a student's academic performance as measured on a regular basis (weekly or monthly). Progress toward meeting the student's goals is measured by comparing expected and actual rates of learning. The information on the student's progress is then used to help the teacher adjust instruction and curriculum to better meet the needs of the student. Thus, the student's progression of achievement is monitored, and instructional techniques are continuously adjusted to meet the individual student's learning needs.

When progress monitoring is implemented correctly, the benefits are great for everyone involved. Benefits include these:

- accelerated learning because students are receiving more appropriate instruction
- more informed instructional decisions
- documentation of student progress for accountability purposes
- more efficient communication with families and other professionals about students' progress
- higher expectations for students by teachers
- fewer special-education referrals

Overall, the use of progress monitoring results in more efficient and appropriately targeted instructional techniques and goals, which together, can improve student attainment of important state standards.

Celebrating Progress

One of the most important ways you can support student learning and help your students raise their expectations of themselves is to celebrate progress as well as achievement. In today's schools, we tend to focus on whether students have achieved a certain standard or goal. That's great, but there are some students for whom that is an impossible benchmark. I (Barbara) used to joke with my students that they couldn't see past the end of their noses to look at our long-term goals (especially the year-end standardized test). If you plan to help your students achieve, you'll need to celebrate each step they make toward a goal.

One way to do this is to have a "Progress Is Power" bulletin board where you can track students' improvements and showcase the progress they are making. In the classrooms we've visited, teachers use anything from train tracks to balloons to graphs to visually represent the progress of their students. We'd offer one caution, though. Make sure the emphasis is on individual progress, not on competing with others.

Phrases to Use with Students to Celebrate Progress

You're on the right track!
That part of your answer is exactly right. Keep going!
You are doing really well.
I'm proud of you for your progress so far.
Have you noticed that you are following directions perfectly? If you keep doing that, you'll finish the assignment successfully.

A Reflective Moment

How do you help your students gauge progress? What are some other phrases you use, or might use, to celebrate their progress?

_____

_____

Summative Assessment

Summative assessment is used to provide a summary of student performance that can be aligned with programs and teaching to provide overall looks. These assessments are typically used periodically as checkpoints on performance.

It's beneficial to provide multiple ways for students to show you how they understand the learning concepts. Kendra Alston, academic facilitator at Kennedy Middle School, shared a lesson she learned during a high school social studies class. She wasn't excited to study the 1920s and 1930s, but her teacher, Mr. Baldwin, told the class he was giving a "show me what you know" final exam. As she explains,

> He didn't care how you showed it, as long as you showed what you knew. I was into theater. So I researched the vaudeville circuit at the time and found Bessie Smith. She was a blues singer who sang in speakeasies, and I learned about the '20s and '30s through her eyes. On the day of the exam, I came in singing and stayed in character (others did essays, etc.). He asked questions and I answered based on what Bessie Smith would have said. It's the only way I got through it.

Another option is to provide structured choices. Diane Owens, a math and science teacher, uses a tic-tac-toe handout with nine different assignments. She varies the activities, and students choose three assignments of greatest interest.

Self-Assessment

When we take time to self-assess through reflection, we increase our own learning. The same is true for our students. They need opportunities for deep learning, and reflection is one of the steps. There are three types of reflection for students: reflecting on what they have learned, reflecting on how they learn, and reflecting on their progress.

Reflecting on What I Have Learned

There are many informal ways to have students reflect on what they have learned. You can do this orally by periodically asking them to turn to a partner and explain what they understand. Or you can ask students to write a classified ad, selling what they learned today in your class. In twenty-five words or fewer, students should describe what they learned and the importance of the learning. They can even price its value. Sometimes I use sticky notes, writing a question or prompt on a poster and asking students to respond individually on a sticky note. Then, I can rearrange the notes in categories and use the responses to guide our class discussion.

We've also seen teachers use journals effectively. Students write entries explaining the main idea they learned in the lesson and questions they still have. These serve as a springboard for review or discussion during the next class. The journal could also be used as a learning log. Every day at the end of class, students write down at least one thing they learned. By the end of the week, they have a list of at least five things they have learned, by the end of the month they have twenty, and so on. This is more authentic than a test and allows students to see and personalize what they are learning.

Providing multiple, authentic opportunities for students to think about what they have learned is the key. The actual format doesn't matter. I like to vary what I do, if for no other reason than to prevent boredom.

Reflecting on How I Learn

Most of the reflection opportunities that students have focus on what they have learned. But it's also important for them to think about *how* they are learning. Math teachers Lindsay Grant and Christy Matkovich incorporate opportunities in which students can reflect on their own learning processes. Students are given the opportunity to rework any problems that were incorrect on a test.

As the graphic organizer on the next page shows, students are also asked to think about their learning by explaining why they missed the original question and why they know they have the correct answer now. As Lindsay explains, the process "makes them think about what they've done and what they did differently or what they are supposed to do." The graphic organizer can be easily adapted for work in any subject area.

Understanding Math Better

Name _____   Date _____

Math Test _____   Teacher _____

Question:

My Original Answer:

My New Solution (you must show your work including all steps):

The Correct Answer:

Why I Missed the Question on the Original Test (circle one):

    I didn't understand the question.

    I thought I had it right.

    I skipped a step.

    I studied this but I forgot.

    I had no clue about this.

    I ran out of time or guessed.

    I made a careless mistake.

Why I Know I Have the Right Answer Now:

Similarly, a self-assessment checklist can help your students think about how they learn. It can also help you design lessons that will connect with your students. A variety of learning style assessments are available, but simply asking your students to think about what they like to do can provide valuable information. This simple checklist for elementary school students is a good starting point.

Self-Assessment Checklist		
	Yes	*No*
I like to learn new things.		
I like to draw.		
I like to read.		
I like to write.		
I like to talk to other people.		
I like to make things.		
I like to wiggle and move around.		

There are also a variety of simple self-assessment checklists for students available on the Internet.

Reflecting on My Progress

Everyone needs an opportunity to reflect on their progress. Without it, we tend to forget that we are making progress! Often, we track the progress of our students through stickers, check marks, or some other form of data collection, but our students need the chance to keep up with their own successes. One way is to have your students keep a "victory list" in the back of their journals or student agendas. A victory list is simply a personal list of successes.

Sample Victory List

♦ I completed the science lab successfully.
♦ I knew the answer when my teacher called on me.
♦ I learned a new strategy for organizing information.
♦ I participated in the volleyball game during physical education.
♦ I used information I learned in math during my after-school job.

The purpose of the victory list is to help us remember what we have accomplished, particularly when things aren't going so well. Over time, it also builds a track record of success for learning.

Avoid the Roadblock!

At times, we are so focused on what students learn that we forget to pay attention to how they learn and monitor successes. It's critical to incorporate all three of the options discussed above within your classroom. As a way to help students become more independent, help them track their own learning styles, mistakes, and successes.

Summary

- ◆ The way in which you assess students can have a tremendous impact on learning.
- ◆ Using various types of formative assessment can identify strengths and weaknesses throughout the learning process, help track student progress, and provide a means for celebrating progress.
- ◆ Summative assessment should be varied to allow each student to show knowledge gained in a way that best suits his or her learning style.
- ◆ Providing opportunities for students to reflect on their own learning is a way of self-assessing, which is crucial in the growth process.

6

Challenges and Opportunities

Throughout this book, we've focused on strategies related to motivating students, holding them to high expectations, supporting their learning, and assessing understanding. Now, we'll turn our attention to three final concerns.

1. Differentiating Instruction
2. Applying Individualized Education Programs
3. Increasing Family Involvement

Differentiating Instruction

In order to differentiate instruction, assessment and expectations must be differentiated. This does not mean expectations will be lowered—just altered. Each standard and learning objective can still be met in a way that utilizes individual learning styles. Let's take a look at an example of differentiation for two math students.

A fourth-grade math teacher, Mrs. Hughes, is teaching a Common Core Number and Operations in Base Ten standard:

CCSS.Math.Content.4.NBT.B.5 Multiply a whole number of up to four digits by a one-digit whole number, and multiply two two-digit numbers, using strategies based on place value and the properties of operations. Illustrate and explain the calculation by using equations, rectangular arrays, and/or area models. (National Governors Association, Council of Chief State School Officers, 2010)

In her class, she has two very different students with disabilities. One student, Brandon, has difficulty adding, while the second, Michelle, can multiply single-digit numbers, but not with fluency. Both are having difficulty with working memory. So, rather than simply showing one way to solve two-by-two-digit multiplication, Mrs. Hughes teaches each student different ways and sets different expectations. For Brandon, she makes him draw an array that indicates which numbers must be multiplied to solve the problem. She sets the expectation that he can set up the problem and name the numbers correctly. Once Brandon sets up the problem, Mrs. Hughes provides feedback to Brandon whether or not he was accurate and why. Then, she shows Brandon how to use a calculator for the multiplication and addition needed to solve the problem. With Michelle, Mrs. Hughes has her set up the problem just like Brandon. However, she makes Michelle solve each multiplication step using pen and paper. Michelle is allowed to use a calculator only to check her work.

 A Reflective Moment

What can you learn from Mrs. Hughes's example?

_____

_____

Differentiated instruction is, in essence, adjusting to the individual needs of a learner (Tomlinson, 2001). This broad definition opens the door to every strategy and idea. However, the process of differentiating is more complex than simply applying every idea known to every situation that arises. Differentiating is adjusting to the needs of the learner to help him or her achieve at his or her highest level. Tomlinson describes three main areas for differentiation: content, process, and product. The focus of each area is that students will not necessarily all get the same education, but rather they will get individually appropriate educations.

1. Content Content differentiation refers to what the student is expected to learn. Based on the strengths and capabilities of the student, content goals need to be set. In a geometry class, most students should be able to solve multistep proofs. However, some students may be able to complete only a few steps, and others may simply be learning a flow of logic for deduction. Teachers will need to set the student expectations of each course and units within the course to best help students learn important information.

Another example related to the Common Core literacy standards is that of synthesizing information. You may have some students who are still working at a level of comparison and contrast. In that case, you would have two different content expectations.

Comparison/Contrast of Two Texts (for those students working at lower levels)	*Synthesis of Two or More Texts* (for those students working at more advanced levels)

2. Process Process differentiation refers to how a student most effectively processes the information. Students may prefer different approaches, from a hands-on lesson to student group work to teacher modeling. Differentiating the process means finding the most effective and efficient means for learning the content, which is not the same for every student.

Process differentiation lends itself to such approaches as station teaching and multisensory instruction. Station teaching requires placing students in small groups and having them rotate through different tasks. One of those tasks should be interaction with the teacher, who will instruct the group of students based on their collective needs. Multisensory instruction is an approach that incorporates as many senses as possible into the learning environment. Rather than focusing on who is a visual learner or an auditory learner, multisensory instruction includes stepwise instruction where students manipulate objects and reason out aloud. Multisensory instructional methods have proven effective through several research studies ranging from Orton-Gillingham reading to Concrete-Representational-Abstract math instruction.

3. Product To differentiate according to the product means to adjust assignments according to the strengths of each student. In many cases, students may be provided options for their product of learning (Bender, 2008). While some students may show their learning best through a test on George Washington, others will find alternatives more effective. The point is to find a way to assess what information the student learned so that he or she can best demonstrate the knowledge acquired.

Sample Product Options

Create a mini-documentary on video.
Write a short story.
Record a podcast.
Draw a mural.
Create a rap.
Write a riddle.

A Reflective Moment

How do you currently differentiate in your classroom? How does the information in this chapter add to your knowledge of differentiation?

_____

_____

Before we leave this topic, let's look at one of our most frequently asked questions: How do I truly differentiate my expectations, without giving up rigor? This is a difficult balance, but you must consider the needs of your individual students. Using Bloom's Taxonomy, we've provided different prompting questions at varying levels. For more advanced students in your classroom, you may start at the highest level; for your students with special needs, start with the lower levels and move to the higher levels. Of course, you will need to use scaffolding to help them move up the levels.

Sample Activities: Volcanoes

Elementary School
Level One: Show the structure of a volcano.
Level Two: Create a volcano with a system of lava tubes that reach the surface.
Level Three: Explain how inactive volcanoes produce earthquakes.

Middle School
Level One: Explain how the movement of Earth's plates can create volcanoes.
Level Two: Analyze the interaction of plate tectonics, earthquakes, and volcanic eruptions.
Level Three: Analyze the steps scientists are using to issue short-term warnings before eruptions. Are they the most effective way to notify residents? If so, why? If not, how could they be improved?

The table on the next page provides a useful template for planning.

Differentiation Planning Template

Standard or Objective:
Lesson Focus or Essential Question:
For Students with Special Needs
Adjustment(s) to Standard or Content Differentiation:
Adjustment(s) to Instruction or Process Differentiation (accommodations and modifications):
Adjustment(s) to Assessment or Product Differentiation:

Applying Individualized Education Programs

An IEP is a written document that describes the services that will be provided to a student with a disability. Over time and legislation, the size and complexity of the IEP document has grown to describe such things as liability indicators and legal reminders. Still, most of the components are specifically designed to aid the child. Components include:

♦ A statement of the child's present level of performance and how the disability impacts his or her education
♦ Annual goals based on academic and school-based functional needs of the student, often broken down into stepwise benchmarks
♦ A timeline of services and expectations for the student
♦ Special and related services given to the student to help him or her achieve (such as speech and language therapy, occupational therapy, etc.)
♦ Accommodations and modifications based on the needs of the student
♦ Transitional support for postsecondary employment and/or continued education (if necessary)

While these are the basics to an IEP, many schools and school districts have varied their forms to meet legal matters that have arisen. In a study of IEP forms from different states, Thompson and colleagues (2001) found additional IEP components, such as:

♦ A statement on how the present level of performance would affect the child's general-education performance
♦ Options for statewide and district-wide assessment involvement
♦ A statement regarding alternate assessment

Despite these additional IEP components and districts working diligently to meet the legal requirements of an IEP, Shriner and Destefano (2003) found that many IEPs do not help teachers guide instruction nor ensure student participation in the general-education curriculum. Thus, it is important to provide all stakeholders with clear expectations and an easy-to-follow format. Also, it may be helpful to hold additional meetings with staff to explain steps with instructional delivery, further general- and special-education collaboration, and check on the progress of implementation.

Differentiation within the IEP

Differentiation for special-needs students should be based on their IEPs. Suzanne Okey, a former teacher, explains, "Think of the IEP as a road map. It should be the result of a huge diagnostic workout that shows holes and significant gaps in learning. Put [your IEPs] in your plan book so you see them every day with all your other goals, objectives, and standards. Cover them as you are teaching higher-level concepts with other students, but don't eliminate higher-order thinking skills for this student."

For example, imagine that you are teaching your students how to write a three-paragraph essay. Sanchez's IEP goal is to write in complete sentences with appropriate capitalization and punctuation. How do you teach this while you are teaching others how to write an essay? Suzanne recommends, "You also want to start building the concept in him that writing is more than three short sentences. You might have him write a topic sentence for each paragraph. That might be the bulk of his essay and he might work on that for a period of weeks, but you don't want him to stay there. It's important to not stop and do a whole separate lesson for him. Don't exclude him from rich discussions; he may be able to take it in but not produce it."

 A Reflective Moment

How does Suzanne's example apply to your classroom?

_____

_____

How Do I Work with IEPs?

Benefits of aligned IEPs include higher expectations, focused and collaborative instruction, and increased exposure to curricular content. In a study by McLaughlin, Nolet, Rhim, and Henderson (1999), special-education teachers indicated that when IEPs were aligned with state standards, students with disabilities had improved exposure to subject matter with focused instruction to meet challenging goals. These researchers also found that collaboration between special- and general-education teachers was greater when they worked with a student with an aligned IEP. When using aligned IEPs, educators tended to focus on high expectations rather than on student deficits (Thompson et al., 2001). In sum, the aligned IEP changed teachers' pedagogy and attitudes to ensure that students with disabilities had access to the general-education curriculum. As students with disabilities gain greater access to state content standards, their test scores should improve and the achievement gap between special education and general education should decrease.

How to Effectively Help Students

Kawana Dobbins, a special-education assessor in Guam (Department of Defense schools), provides the following suggestions for helping students with their special needs: "At the beginning of the school year, I meet with all students in ninth grade who have an IEP to discuss their goals and objectives for the school year as well as classroom/testing accommodations. I let them know who their case manager is and their room number so they will know who to contact if a situation arises. In many cases, I also have to explain what an IEP is and/or what their disability is and what it means to them. By addressing these issues upfront, I tend to see more cooperation out of students because they know what is going on with them and they know they have the support needed to help them be successful in the classroom."

 ## A Reflective Moment

What is the most important point from the section above about IEPs?

_____

_____

Components of Effective IEPs

Who. The IEP team is the group of stakeholders who are responsible for the education and well-being of the student. I (Brad) have attended IEP meetings with peers, parent advocates, lawyers, coaches, and clergy. All these people were welcomed to their respective meetings and included in being responsible for meeting goals.

At a minimum, the people who should attend are:

♦ The child (unless the meeting is contentious)
♦ Parents and/or guardians
♦ General-education teachers per subject matter
♦ Special-education teachers involved
♦ A psychologist or someone else who can discuss assessment results and what they mean to the child's schooling
♦ Education leader who understands district policies and can make decisions about resources
♦ Transition-service representative (depending on age), such as vocational counselor to talk about the postsecondary needs of the student and resources available

What. As stated earlier, the focus of an IEP is to determine measurable goals for a student. Having high expectations for a student is important, but having unrealistic ones may frustrate the student and parents and cause undue paperwork when making the corrections. It is important to base goals on data learned from formative and summative assessments. Also, chart student growth through the goals to progress from one step in the learning process to the next. For example, if a fifth-grade student is weak at whole-number multiplication but we are trying to have him learn decimal multiplication, I may write a goal as follows:

> Given two-digit decimal multiplication problems on a test, Marissa will complete them with at least 80 percent accuracy.

However, because she is not ready to do this yet, if the form permits, I write state benchmarks that progress to meeting this goal. For example:

1.1 Given single-digit multiplication problems on a fluency probe, Brad will complete at least 15 in a minute with 100 percent accuracy by the end of the first grading period.
1.2 Given up to 10 two-digit multiplication problems on a test, Brad will use an array to solve problems with 100 percent accuracy by the end of the second grading period.
1.3 Given single-digit decimal multiplication problems on a fluency probe, Brad will complete at least 10 in a minute with 90 percent accuracy by the end of the third grading period.
1.4 Given up to 10 two-digit decimal multiplication problems on a test, Brad will use an array to solve them with at least 90 percent accuracy by the end of the school year.

The format of the goal and benchmarks should be clear enough to follow for a teacher to observe and measure the behavior. Also, a strategy was named, arrays, in leading to the outcome. Having an observable and measurable outcome along with a named instructional strategy lends itself to more consistent delivery and instructional integrity.

Why. IEP teams meet not only because it is the law but because an IEP clearly describes special services that assist the student's learning and the individual responsibilities within a team to assess student achievement in meeting educationally relevant goals.

 Three Possible Roadblocks

1. What do I do if a student does not appear to be progressing toward a particular IEP goal?

Document the student's work regarding the appropriate goal using progress monitoring and formative assessment. Document what you have done to help the student achieve. Seek other educators' advice, and review research-supported strategies that pertain to the goal and the student's situation. If those prove to be unsuccessful, then it is necessary to reconvene the IEP team to determine the appropriateness of the goal and possible accommodations and modifications to help the student achieve.

2. A student appears to be inconsistent in his or her achievement from class to class or from school to home. What can we do to help with the consistency?

First, inconsistency is normal in all of us and, to some extent, should be expected. However, sustained differences in performance, based on specific environments, requires further investigation. Research has been conducted on student performance based on the consistency and accuracy of teachers implementing the IEP requirements. When using read-alouds as a test accommodation, teachers are required to read word problems out loud for the student to process by listening rather than by reading. If one teacher reads the word problems in a monotone voice with even spacing between words and sentences but another teacher emphasizes key words and checks for understanding during the read-aloud, the student will likely perform differently between the two teachers. Likewise, if a behavior plan is set with scripted responses and specific actions according to a student's behavior but a parent or rogue teacher does not follow through with the plan consistently, the student may act differently in different situations or even confuse the consequences, thus undermining the effectiveness of the behavior intervention. Before inconsistency becomes an issue, teach the procedures, check for clarity, and have all IEP team members sign that they will comply according to the directions. Then, develop a system for assessing implementation fidelity.

3. How do I get the student more involved in the education process?

The purpose of the IEP is the betterment of the student. Thus, the student should be present during meetings and, whenever possible, should be involved in the development of the IEP and even lead the IEP discussion during the annual meeting. Student IEP participation is done throughout the country with many students with disabilities and is now encouraged legally. McGahee-Kovac (2002) pioneered student-led IEPs, describing how to prepare students for meetings, what they should do during meetings, and how to monitor the students' ongoing self-determinism following meetings. Since McGahee-Kovac's efforts, organizations have stepped forward to help educators and parents through the process.

A Reflective Moment

How does this section change your view of IEPs? Are there ways you can use IEPs more effectively with your students? Do you still have questions about their use?

_____

_____

Increasing Family Involvement

Family involvement, from attending meetings to volunteering in school, declines as a student maintains a special-education label. Additionally, the lower the family income, the less likely families will be involved at school (Special Education Elementary Longitudinal Study, SRI, 2001). Generally, parent attendance in parent training and support meetings is historically low as well. However, we know that family involvement helps with overall student learning. For this reason, educators must create avenues for families to feel comfortable and safe so they begin to develop a trusting relationship with the school.

 A Reflective Moment

What is your biggest challenge related to family involvement with your special-needs students?

_____

_____

Individualized Family Service Plan

When a child is diagnosed with a disability early in life, the child and his or her family is provided services according to their Individualized Family Service Plan (IFSP). The IFSP is a document that describes the strengths and needs of the child, the disability diagnosis, a timeline for when the child should meet some expected outcomes, and who is responsible. The team meets annually so that the child may continue to grow and develop in the home and be monitored as to the effectiveness of the services. The IFSP exists for children from birth to age three, when an Individualized Education Program (IEP) begins. An IEP has similar components except that it focuses more so on what is educationally relevant to the child. Still, make no mistake, the IEP is as family oriented as the IFSP. Both the IEP and IFSP require multidisciplinary teams, including the family, to make decisions in the best interest of the child. After all, what is in the best interest of the child is of the utmost concern to parents.

Other Strategies

Make family connections different and dynamic. Legally, we must include families as part of the IEP team, but you can take it further than this. Show families how to monitor student performance at home or provide student-led IEPs and student-led back-to-school nights using the following guidelines:

- ◆ Make sessions short (twenty minutes max).
- ◆ Enjoy the time and make it positive.
- ◆ Incorporate high child involvement.

Keep in mind parents may not know how to help their child at home. You might suggest they keep a running record or a log of what they observe, reteach and/or support the class lesson, and notify you when they teach something new at home. Depending on the parents and their trust level with you, you will find varying levels of support. Also, when you meet with them on a regular basis, remember they have a different perspective on their son or daughter than you do. It's helpful to "take A LAP" during meetings.

Take A LAP

- ◆ Accept that parents may have a different opinion on their child.
- ◆ Listen to ideas and complaints without judgment.
- ◆ Ask questions to clarify.
- ◆ Positive endings continue relationships.

You also want to avoid barriers to communication when working with parents. Watch your educational vocabulary. Parents do not want to be intimidated or feel threatened by educational jargon. Explain everything, but do it in a way that reaches your audience while showing compassion first and foremost. Take extra precautions to not place blame anywhere; rather, use the word *we* whenever talking about plans for the student, to imply a team effort between school and family. Finally, avoid labeling the child. Simply provide observations and quantitative data without drawing conclusions that can damage the relationship you have worked to build. After all, you are talking about a child that the parents love and cherish. Insert hope and optimism as much as possible. It'll go a long way in building trust.

Lower-income parents may be particularly sensitive to your reactions to their suggestions. Many times, they have had negative experiences with schools. Brad worked with two low-income parents, and they suggested he work with their daughter in a particular manner. When he accepted their suggestion and implemented it, they cried because "the school never listened before." Despite the guise of a prickly shield, most parents are insecure about their parenting, particularly when the labels of failure are placed on their children.

 Avoid the Roadblock!

Remember that parents simply want their sons and daughters to be successful. This means at times they will push you to be more helpful or supportive. Don't take it personally! Also, parents may be intimidated by your language or even your presence. For some parents, school is a negative experience; therefore they come in with that perspective. Be positive and look at parent involvement as a partnership that at times may be stressful but in the end will make a difference for the student.

 Summary

- ♦ In order to differentiate instruction, assessment and expectations must be differentiated.
- ♦ An Individualized Education Program provides a road map for how a student will learn best, according to his or her strengths and weaknesses.
- ♦ Family involvement can be a critical factor in maximizing the success of your students with disabilities. Make family connections dynamic.

Conclusion

Students with disabilities too often are viewed merely as students in trouble. View students with disabilities as children with unique abilities that may or may not have been discovered yet. For those of us who teach, this means we must adjust how we teach to meet those needs and find those abilities. It is our hope that, as you have journeyed through this book, you have found new ideas and perhaps have been reminded of some other ideas that will help your students. We believe that teachers are the most powerful force in student learning. Thank you for all you do.

Teachers are the true superheroes of America. They are talented and energetic people, capable of making incredible changes in society. Due to a moral obligation that few understand, they use their talents for the good of others. They spend long hours in preparation and presentation, coaching and leading to improve the lives of young children, who can carry forth their altruistic message. Their multiplicative powers extend from the students in their class to every person that each student comes in contact with. To make such change requires the differentiation of individual needs of students while ensuring that everyone reaches academic benchmarks. Teachers play such roles as commander, leader, partner, facilitator, cheerleader, and officer in situations where each is needed. While using their talents and efforts in order to help others, they sacrifice money, family time, and personal desires. They seldom receive thanks, commensurate salaries, or tangible rewards. More recently, some have even received admonishment for their extreme efforts with those who struggle the most if standardized assessment scores are not favorable. Many of the complaints have even come from those who benefitted from similar efforts. I've seen teachers approached negatively by parents for giving an honest grade, by administrators because they taught a social skill rather than a standard, and even by their own family members for choosing teaching as a career.

Why would people choose such a life? Only Spider-Man and Superman would understand. Why would someone dare to be a teacher in today's economic and social climate? Why? A teacher's salary isn't going to buy a huge home, a luxury car, or private jet. What teachers do make, however, is a difference. Teaching is a job designed to change the world. Without teachers, where would anyone be? As Richard Riley said, education is the career that makes all other careers possible. Please, we urge you, the next time you see a teacher, unmasked, at the store, stop and thank him or her. For teachers are the superheroes of today and deserve to be treated as such.

Suggestions for Using *Rigor for Students with Special Needs* with Book Clubs or Study Groups

Effective Staff Development

While working on her doctorate, Barbara studied schools that had won a national award for their staff development (Blackburn, 2000). From that, she learned there are seven key elements of effective staff development.

Key Elements of Effective Staff Development

1. Clear purpose linked to research, student data, goals, and needs
2. Accountability through classroom use of ideas and impact on students
3. Development of a common, shared language
4. Shared decision making that includes an emphasis on teacher input
5. Incorporation of relevant, practical, hands-on activities
6. Integration of opportunities for follow-up and application
7. Strong leadership and a positive, collegial atmosphere

Book clubs and study groups are an effective component of a staff development program. Hopefully, you have chosen to study *Rigor for Students with Special Needs* because it matches a need or goal in your school. Through a book study, your faculty will develop a common, shared language and perspective of rigor, which can serve as a foundation for future growth. Through the portions in the book labeled "A Reflective Moment" and the suggestions provided below, you can incorporate hands-on activities for follow-up that will also allow for accountability through classroom use of the material. Finally, through the leadership of the faculty and administrators in your building, you will be able to tailor the material to the specific needs of your students, in order to maximize learning.

General Suggestions

Teachers may benefit from discussing ideas and concerns by chapter. If you are a facilitator or member of a book club or study group, you may want to hold roundtable discussions after the chapters to help faculty build on one another's ideas. This will also help in establishing or implementing schoolwide initiatives, as each teacher will have input and ownership over the strategies discussed. Barbara has this facilitator's guide posted on her website, along with free downloads from the book. Keep in mind there are chapter-specific questions in each "A Reflective Moment" section. There is also a summary at the end of each chapter. Please consider that many of the questions ask teachers to analyze their own behaviors and practices with a critical eye; therefore, unless there is an atmosphere of trust in your group, some teachers may be less willing to share that information publicly.

Overall Guiding Questions and Activities

The first set of activities below are divided into three sections: pre-reading activities, for teachers to complete prior to reading the book; during-reading activities, which can be used anytime during the discussions; and after-reading activities, to be completed after teachers have finished the book. The ideas are purposely generic. Balance the use of these with the more specific suggestions throughout the book to best meet the needs of your particular situation and/or group.

Prereading Activities

Sentence Starters
Write the following phrases on chart paper. Post them around the room, and ask teachers to anonymously respond to each using Post-it notes. Group each set of notes by category, and use them as discussion starters.

Rigor is . . .
Rigor is not . . .
The biggest challenge to working with students who have special needs in our school is . . .
I wish . . .

Find the Solution!

On an index card, each person writes one of the biggest classroom or student-specific challenges he or she is facing related to rigor. Fold each card, and place it in a bowl. Each group member then chooses a challenge from the bowl. As you progress through the chapters, look for solutions to those challenges. After reading the book in its entirety, everyone will share the index-card challenges they drew, as well as the solutions they found in the book.

Pipe-Cleaner Responses

Each teacher uses a pipe cleaner to form a shape that represents how his or her students respond to the notion of rigor or challenging work. Ask each to share the shape with the group and explain it.

During-Reading Activities

Learning Walk

As you begin to implement some of the strategies, do a learning walk. Find other teachers who are willing, and visit one another's classrooms. Look for examples of rigor, motivation, and engagement. Discuss the positive examples you see.

Write a Letter to a New Teacher

Write a letter to a first-year teacher using the following terms:

Rigor Intrinsic Motivation Diagnostic Assessment
Extrinsic Motivation Concrete-Representational-Abstract
Accommodation Modification Scaffolding
Myth

My Head Is Spinning!

Draw two heads: one smiling and one with a question mark. In the smiling head, write ideas from the book that you connect with. In the one with a question mark, write questions you have from each chapter.

Try It Out!

Choose at least three strategies discussed in the book. Implement them individually, and then discuss in the book group.

After-Reading Activities

Author Interview

Write a list of interview questions or a letter in which you ask the authors a series of questions about some of the ideas expressed in the book.

Sharing Our Successes

Have each teacher take a picture of the student work that resulted from one of the strategies suggested in the book. Then, ask the teacher to write what he or she learned from the activity. Create a bulletin board in the faculty workroom or lounge to showcase student and teacher learning!

Blueprint for Literacy

Work together in small groups to create a blueprint for increasing rigor for your students with special needs. Include the next steps and any needed tools or resources.

APPENDIX B

Blackline Masters

Ways to Add Value to Instruction

V	Variety	Include a variety of activities, assignments, projects, etc. Have a structure, but don't get caught up in a boring routine.
A	Attractiveness	Integrate elements of movement, curiosity, and originality into your lessons.
L	Locus of control	To address students' need for some control over their circumstances or ownership in the learning, provide opportunities for them to be a part of the learning experience, rather than simply being told what to do.
U	Utility	Students need to see the utility, purpose, or relevance of the lesson. Provide real-life connections.
E	Enjoyment	Students are more motivated when they find pleasure in what they are doing. Although you need to have a classroom with structure and order, that may look different in different classrooms. It is absolutely, positively OK to smile and have fun. Play games, make jokes, and do something different.

Set Goals and Expectations

Goal	Student's Job	Teacher's Job	Reward for Meeting Goal

1. Determine if learned helplessness exists.

2. Explicitly model the preferred academic behavior.

3. Teach the student a strategy for displaying the preferred academic behavior.

4. Provide practice for the strategy.

5. Set a cue to remind the student to initiate the strategy.

6. Allow the student to succeed.

7. Facilitate the student's problem-solving strategy.

Questioning Bookmark

How would I feel or react?

Does this make sense?
Why did I think that?

How would my friends react to
this? Would my friends do this?

How does this compare to . . . ?
What would I change?

How does the picture help me?
What does the subheading mean?

Question Matrix

What Is	When Is	Where Is	Which Is	Who Is	Why Is	How Is
What Did	When Did	Where Did	Which Did	Who Did	Why Did	How Did
What Can	When Can	Where Can	Which Can	Who Can	Why Can	How Can
What Would	When Would	Where Would	Which Would	Who Would	Why Would	How Would
What Will	When Will	Where Will	Which Will	Who Will	Why Will	How Will
What Might	When Might	Where Might	Which Might	Who Might	Why Might	How Might

Source: Wiederhold (1995).

Flesh It Out

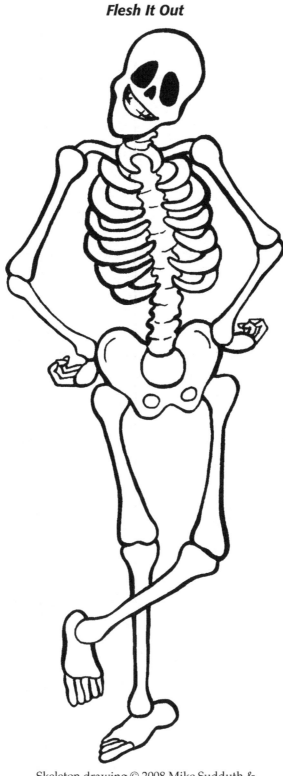

Skeleton drawing © 2008 Mike Sudduth &
Carlee Lingerfelt. Used with permission.

T-Chart

Planning Graphic Organizer

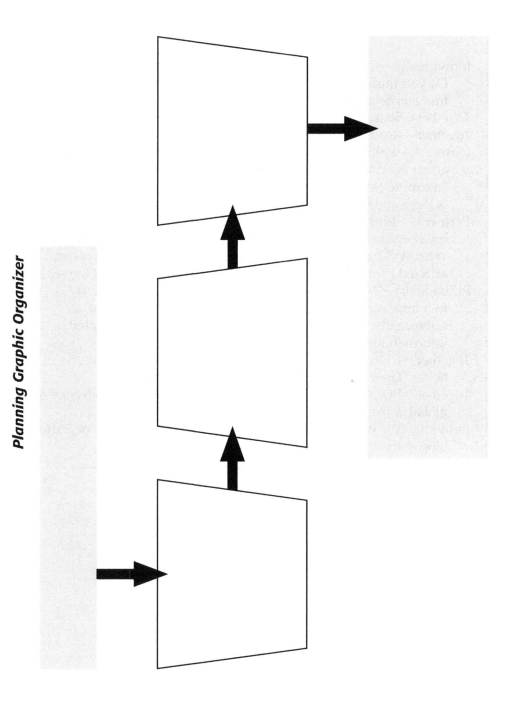

Interactive Reading Guide

Write Time for Kids
"Earth's Baffling Climate Machine"

Individually—Quickly write down your thoughts on Earth's climate. Do you think it's getting warmer? Why or why not? Do you think humans need to change their ways?

Together—Share your thoughts.

Together—Read the expository piece on the Earth's rising climate.

Partner A—Phil Jones makes an interesting statement. When asked about the cause of the warming climate, he says that it is not "a simple case of either-or." What do you think he means by that? Is there another phrase you would use to describe his perspective?

Partner B—Tom Wigley makes a statement about the visibility of rising sea levels. What effect will that have on your everyday life? What will happen if the sea levels rise quickly? Whose lives will be affected the most? How might this affect the creatures of the sea?

Individually—Make connections with what you have just read to information on global warming that the media has put out recently. Use the Internet or newspapers to find updated information.

Together—Discuss what you found. Is the situation getting worse or better? Create a visual that explains your perspective.

Together—Brainstorm ideas on how humanity can attempt to combat global warming.

Individually—Write a letter to the editor of your local paper or write a blog entry about your opinion.

Student Cooperative Learning Rubric

	You're a Team Player 3	You're Working on It... 2	You're the Lone Ranger 1	Total for Each Category
G Group Dedication	I listened respectfully to my teammates' ideas and offered suggestions that helped my group.	I did listen to ideas, but I didn't give suggestions.	I was distracted and more interested in the other groups than my group.	**Group Dedication** I circled number 3 2 1
R Responsibility	I eagerly accepted responsibility with my group and tried to do my part to help everyone in my group.	I accepted responsibility within my group without arguing.	I quarreled and did not accept roles given by my group.	**Responsibility** I circled number 3 2 1
O Open Communication	I listened to others' ideas and tried to solve conflicts peacefully.	I listened to others' ideas, but did not try to solve conflicts.	I was controlling and argumentative to my group.	**Open Communication** I circled number 3 2 1
U Use of Work Time	I was involved and engaged; I encouraged my group the entire time we were working.	I tried my best the entire time we were working.	I was not involved and did not offer any suggestions for the good of the group.	**Use of Work Time** I circled number 3 2 1
P Participation	I was a team member. I offered ideas, suggestions, and help for my group.	I participated in the project, but did not offer to help anyone.	I did not participate because I was not interested.	**Participation** I circled number 3 2 1
				Total _____

Understanding Math Better

Name _____ Date _____

Math Test _____ Teacher _____

Question:

My Original Answer:

My New Solution (you must show your work including all steps):

The Correct Answer:

Why I Missed the Question on the Original Test (circle one):

   I didn't understand the question.

   I thought I had it right.

   I skipped a step.

   I studied this but I forgot.

   I had no clue about this.

   I ran out of time or guessed.

   I made a careless mistake.

Why I Know I Have the Right Answer Now:

Self-Assessment Checklist

	Yes	No
I like to learn new things.		
I like to draw.		
I like to read.		
I like to write.		
I like to talk to other people.		
I like to make things.		
I like to wiggle and move around.		

Differentiation Planning Template

Standard or Objective:	
Lesson Focus or Essential Question:	
For Students with Special Needs	
Adjustment(s) to Standard or Content Differentiation:	
Adjustment(s) to Instruction or Process Differentiation (accommodations and modifications):	
Adjustment(s) to Assessment or Product Differentiation:	

Rigor Bookmark

Cut out this bookmark and use it as a reminder of what rigor really is.

Front   Back

Rigor Made EASY		Myths About Rigor	
E	**E**ngages all students	1	Lots of homework is a sign of rigor.
A	**A**ccommodates all learners	2	Rigor means doing more.
S	**S**caffolds learning	3	Rigor is not for everyone.
Y	**Y**ields results	4	Providing support means lessening rigor.
		5	Resources equal rigor.

Tic-Tac-Toe

You must choose any three assignments Tic-Tac-Toe fashion and complete one assignment each week for the next three weeks. The first will be due on _____ , the next on _____ , and the last on _____ . These will be your problems of the week for the next three weeks, so choose wisely.

I understand that I am to complete one project each week for the next three weeks.

Signature _____   Date _____

Text-to-Text Connection Guide

Today's Story or Text:

Connects to

Other Stories or Books I've Read	Something in One of My Textbooks	A Newspaper, Magazine, or Internet Article

Connections Chart

My connections after reading _____

T (text to other text)	S (text to myself)	W (text to my world)

Guided Notes

Cause/Effect, Logical Order, and Compare and Contrast

Two _____ are related as _____ and
_____ if one brings about or _____
the other. The event that happens _____, is the
_____. The event that happens _____,
is the _____.

Cause/Effect Signal Words

Comparison

To point out what _____ or _____
things have in _____ is to make a _____.
Writers use _____ to make _____
and details _____ to readers.

Contrast

To _____ is to point out _____
between things. _____
_____
_____ _____

Organizing Word Problems

Clue Words

What I Know K	**Question** ?	**Steps to Solve**
	Anything Missing? ▲	

Write a sentence explaining the solution. S

Reproduced with permission from Blackburn and Witzel, *Rigor for Students with Special Needs*. Copyright 2014 Eye On Education

LISTEN Bookmark

Front

Back

References

The Access Center. (2004). *Aligning IEPs with state standards and accountability systems.* Retrieved from the Montana Office of Public Instruction website: http://opi.mt.gov/pub/CSPD/AligningIEPswithStateStandards.pdf

Allen, J. (2004). *Yellow brick roads: Shared and guided paths to independent reading 4–12.* Portland, ME: Stenhouse.

Ames, C. (1992). Classrooms: Goals, structures, and student motivation. *Journal of Educational Psychology, 84,* 261–271.

Bender, W. N. (2008). *Differentiating instruction for students with learning disabilities.* (2nd ed.). Thousand Oaks, CA: Corwin.

Blackburn, B. (2000). *Barriers and facilitators to effective staff development: Perceptions from award-winning practitioners.* Unpublished doctoral dissertation, University of North Carolina at Greensboro, Greensboro.

Blackburn, B. *(2008).Rigor is not a four-letter word.* Larchmont, NY: Eye On Education.

Bruner, J. (1960). *The process of education.* Cambridge, MA: Harvard University Press.

Dweck, C. S., & Elliott, E. S. (1983). Achievement motivation. In P. Mussen & E. M. Hetherington (Eds.), *Handbook of child psychology* (pp. 643–691). New York, NY: Wiley.

Ellis, E. S. (1991). *Slant: A starter strategy for class participation.* Lawrence, KA: Edge Enterprises.

Hollenbeck, K., Tindal, G., & Almond, P. (1998). Teachers' knowledge of accommodations as a validity issue in high-stakes testing. *The Journal of Special Education, 32*(3), 175–183.

Kemp, S. E. (2006). Dropout policies and trends for students with and without disabilities. *Adolescence, 41* (162), 235-250.

Maag, J. W. (2001). Rewarded by punishment: Reflections on the disuse of positive reinforcement in schools. *Exceptional Children, 67,* 173–186.

McDonnell, L. M., McLaughlin, M. J., & Morison, P. (Eds.). (1997). *Educating one and all: Students with disabilities and standards-based reform.* Washington, DC: National Academies Press.

McGahee-Kovac, M. (2002). A student's guide to the IEP. *LDOnline.* Retrieved from http://www.ldonline.org/article/A_Student%27s_Guide_to_the_IEP/5944

McIntosh, K., Goodman, S., & Bohanan, H. (2010). Toward true integration of academic and behavior response to intervention systems, part one: Tier 1 support. *Communiqué, 39*(2), 1, 14–16.

McLaughlin, M. J., Nolet, V., Rhim, L. M., & Henderson, K. (1999). Integrating standards, including all students. *Teaching Exceptional Children, 31*(3), 66–71.

National Governors Association Center for Best Practices, Council of Chief State School Officers. (2010). *Common Core State Standards.* Washington, DC: National Governors Association Center for Best Practices, Council of Chief State School Officers.

Office of Juvenile Justice and Delinquency Prevention. (1995). *Juvenile offenders and victims: A national report.* Pittsburgh, PA: National Center for Juvenile Justice.

Pitt, T. (2003, November 18). Charles Schwab didn't let dyslexia stop him. *USA Today.* Retrieved from http://usatoday30.usatoday.com/money/companies/management/2003-11-10-schwab_x.htm

Schultz, W., Tremblay, L., & Hollerman, J. R. (2000). Reward processing in primate orbitofrontal cortex and basal ganglia. *Cerebral Cortex, 10*(3), 272–284.

Settle, S. A., & Milich, R. (1999). Social persistence following failure in boys and girls with LD. *Journal of Learning Disabilities, 32,* 201–212.

Shapiro, S. (1993). Strategies that create a positive classroom climate. *The Clearing House, 67*(2), 91–97.

Shriner, J. G., & DeStefano, L. (2003). Participation and accommodation in state assessment: The role of individualized education programs. *Council for Exceptional Children, 69*(2), 147–161.

Sinclair, M. F., Christenson, S. L., Evelo, D. L., & Hurley, C. M. (1998). Dropout prevention for youth with disabilities: Efficacy of a sustained school engagement procedure. *Exceptional Children, 65*(1), 7–21.

Skinner, E. A., & Belmont, M. J. (1993). Motivation in the classroom: Reciprocal effects of teacher behavior and student engagement across the school year. *Journal of Educational Psychology, 85*(4), 571–581.

SRI International (2010). *Special Education Elementary Longitudinal Study.* Retrieved at http://www.seels.net/grindex.html

Sprick, R., Garrison, M., & Howard, L. (1998). *Champs: A proactive and positive approach to classroom management.* Longmont, CO: Sopris West.

Thompson, S. J., Thurlow, M. L., Quenemoen, R. F., Esler, A., & Whetstone, P. (2001). *Addressing standards and assessment on state IEP forms* (NCEO Synthesis Report 38). Minneapolis: University of Minnesota, National Center on Educational Outcomes. Retrieved from http://education.umn.edu/NCEO/OnlinePubs/Synthesis38.html

Thurlow, M. L., Sinclair, M. F., & Johnson, D. R. (2002). Students with disabilities who drop out of school—Implications for policy and practice. *NCSET Issue Brief, 1* (2). Retrieved from http://www.ncset.org/publications/viewdesc.asp?id=425

Tomlinson, C. A. (2001). *How to differentiate instruction in mixed-ability classrooms* (2nd ed.). Alexandria, VA: Association for Supervision and Curriculum Development.

U.S. Department of Education, National Center for Education Statistics. (2001). *Dropout rates in the United States: 2000,* NCES 2002-114. Washington, DC: Author.

Vygotsky, L. S. (1978). *Mind and society: The development of higher mental processes.* Cambridge, MA: Harvard University Press.

Wagner, A. D. (1999). Working memory contributions to human learning and remembering. *Neuron, 22,* 19–22. Retrieved from http://web.mit .edu/wagner/www/papers/WAG_NEURON99.pdf

Wasserstein, P. (1995). What middle schoolers say about their schoolwork. *Educational Leadership, 53,* 41–43.

Weiderhold, C. (1995). *Cooperative learning and higher level thinking: The Q-Matrix.* San Clemente, CA: Kagan.

Witzel, B. S. (2007). Using contingent praise to engage students in inclusive classrooms. *Teachers as Leaders, 7,* 27–32.

Witzel, B. S., & Mercer, C. D. (2003). Applying rewards to teach students with disabilities: Implications for motivation. *Remedial and Special Education, 24,* 88–96.

28879544R00072

Made in the USA
Columbia, SC
18 October 2018